In the Heart of France

In the Heart of France

THE DORDOGNE

Text by **Simon Cobley**

Photographs by **David Gallant**

CLARKSON POTTER/PUBLISHERS
NEW YORK

Published by Clarkson N. Potter, Inc., 201 East 50th Street, New
York, New York 10022

Originally published in Great Britain by George Weidenfeld &
Nicolson Ltd. in 1990.

CLARKSON N. POTTER, POTTER, and colophon are
trademarks of Clarkson N. Potter, Inc.

Manufactured in Italy

Library of Congress Cataloguing-in-Publication Data
is available upon request
ISBN 0-517-58126-4
10 9 8 7 6 5 4 3 2 1

First American Edition

Endpapers: Château de Puymartin, near Sarlat
Half-title page: Near Saint-Vivien
Title page: The Dordogne from Domme

CONTENTS

A field of buttercups provides a
striking contrast to the woods
and vineyards surrounding the
tiny Romanesque church of
Saint-Nexans, near Bergerac.

Map of the Dordogne area
showing the location of places
illustrated in this book.

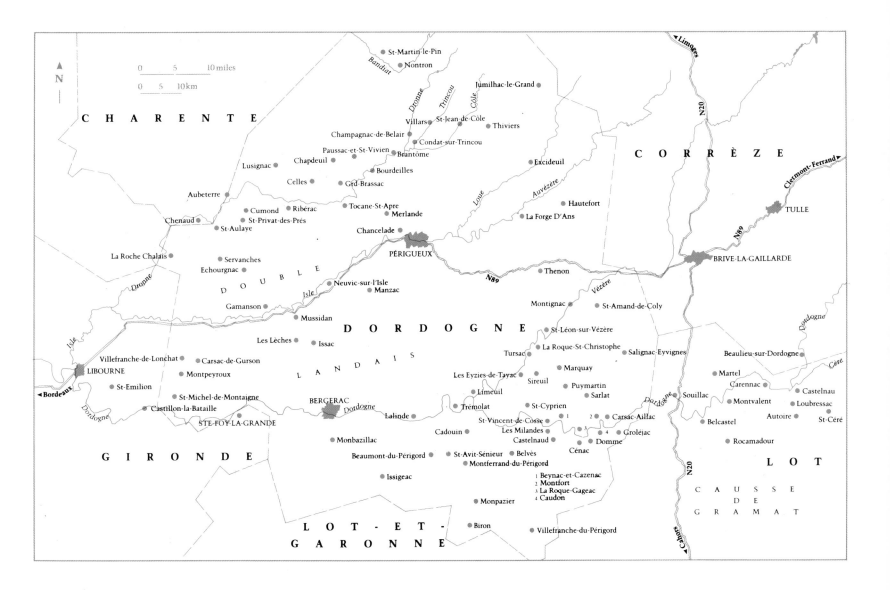

INTRODUCTION

**CHÂTEAU DE
CASTELNAUD**

The twelfth-century Château
de Castelnaud stands –
surrounded by woodland – on a
promontory, directly across
the Dordogne from Château
Beynac, a thousand feet above
the river at its confluence with
the Céou. Originally belonging
to the Cazenac family it was
briefly occupied in 1214 by
Simon de Montfort, father of
the English ruler, during the
Albigensian Crusade. Falling
into the hands of the French, it
was retaken in 1407 by the
English and fortified. During
the Hundred Years War
Castelnaud was an English
stronghold, ideally situated for
keeping the rival French-held
Château Beynac under
observation; the fields and
meadows between the two
châteaux were often the scene
of bloody skirmishes. The
château had since been
allowed to fall into disrepair,
but a scheme of restoration is
now under way.

The Dordogne, arguably France's best-loved river, rises high in the Massif Central at
the peak of the Puy de Sancy. It probably takes its name from the Celtic Dur-unna,
meaning rapid waters, rather than the union of two streams, the Dore and the Dogne.
The river flows swiftly southwest for three hundred miles where it combines briefly
with the Garonne to form the Gironde estuary before meeting the Atlantic at Bordeaux. On its journey to the sea the river passes through a landscape of immense diversity, largely unspoilt by modern farming methods or by the inevitable tourism that a
region of such natural and man-made beauty will attract.

The river gives its name to the administrative region of Dordogne, one of France's
ninety-five *départements*. The ancient territory of Périgord was renamed Dordogne at
the time of the Revolution, but the new boundaries of the *département* – formed for
local government purposes – correspond closely with those of the former province,
and the terms Dordogne and Périgord are, to all intents and purposes, synonymous.
Links with the distant past die hard in this region and the inhabitants resolutely refer
to themselves as *Périgordin* and never *Dordognais*; to them the Dordogne is the name
of their delightful river and its adoption by bureaucrats from outside is merely con-
sidered as a term of reference for their own convenience, no more.

The modern *département* lies, landlocked, east of the Atlantic coast and north of
the valley of the Lot. It is almost diamond-shaped with its four corners stretching
towards Limoges in the north, Montauban in the south, Bordeaux in the west and
Brive in the east. At its centre lies Périgueux, the present-day capital, once the capital
of ancient Périgord.

To appreciate the region to the full it is necessary to have a rudimentary grasp of its
complex history. Recorded history begins when the Romans came to the region in
56 B.C. but the wealth of prehistoric remains is evidence that the Dordogne has been
continuously inhabited for thousands of years. Around the village of Les Eyzies on the

River Vézère many traces of Palaeolithic habitations have been found. The artefacts and cave paintings, primitive shelters and graves, and, above all, the momentous discovery in the nineteenth century of the skeletons of Cro-Magnon man have justly given the village the title of 'Capital of Prehistory'. The chance discovery a hundred years later of the now world-famous painted caves at Lascaux has confirmed the importance of the region in the study of prehistory.

Périgord has four principal rivers and, before the advent of the Romans, the region was inhabited by four tribes, whose respective territories were probably founded in the four river valleys. These four Celtic clans, known as the Petro-corii, from which Périgord takes its name, had the settlement at Vesunna on the river Isle as their territorial headquarters. Under Roman occupation the settlement was developed and renamed Vesunna Augusta; this would later become Périgueux. Evidence of Roman influence is not very apparent in the Dordogne but the most substantial remains are to be found at Périgueux. The Romans, under Augustus, gave the area as a whole the name of Aquitania, the Land of Waters, a name which persists today as Aquitaine. More significantly they introduced the walnut, chestnut and the grapevine, laying the foundations for centuries of agricultural life, a life which continues to this day.

In the third century the constant threat of invasion by barbarian hordes became a reality; Teutonic Franks from the north and Alamans from beyond the Rhine poured into Gaul. Roman Gaul went into a decline and, as wave after wave of barbarian invasions swept across the region, the administration collapsed. In the fifth century the Visigoths occupied Aquitaine and spread south to Provence finally dismembering Roman Gaul.

Christianity had been introduced in the third century and under Clovis, who led the Teutonic Franks to displace the Visigoths, it came to dominate and unite the region. It was under Clovis, who had converted to Christianity in AD 496, that the *regnum Francorum* (the kingdom of the Franks) was established. After his death in AD 551 the Merovingian dynasty collapsed; the region slid into a state of continuous factional fighting and dispute, and was united only by a common-held belief in Christianity. Successive invasions had led to a great depopulation and Périgord became completely covered by forest. These uninhabited regions were attractive to hermits; a number of villages like Saint-Amand-de-Coly and Saint-Avit-Sénieur still bear their names, and many of the former Gallo-Roman villas left intact by the barbarians became the first monasteries at this time.

In the eighth century the whole country was united against the threat of the Saracens who invaded from Spain to meet defeat at the hands of Charles Martel at Poitiers in AD 732. Charles Martel's grandson, Charles the Great or Charlemagne, united the Christian kingdoms of the West to form the Holy Roman Empire. Christianity flourished in Périgord under Charlemagne, and he supported the establishment of the economically powerful Benedictine monasteries. The relative peace in the region died when he died, however. Invasions by the Northmen, who sacked Bordeaux and then Périgueux, left a trail of destruction along the rivers, which gave access to the inland settlements. Churches and monasteries were pillaged and destroyed, yet faith in Christianity was left unshaken. In the latter half of the ninth century there was a great resurgence in ecclesiastical building and over the period of the next two hundred years over a thousand churches, abbeys and other religious buildings sprang up in Périgord in the style of architecture that we call Romanesque. Coinciding with this ecclesiastical expansion and the spread of monasticism there was a resettlement of the rural areas. Hamlets and villages grew up – often around the monasteries – whose inhabitants were dependent upon a system of polyculture and vineyards for their subsistence and upon the feudal lords for their protection.

The history of the Dordogne is dominated by the Hundred Years War, itself only a part of a continuous conflict spanning three centuries. In 1137 Eleanor, daughter of Duke Guillaume x who had no male heir, was married to Louis VII, the future King of France, thus uniting the French crown with the powerful Duchy of Aquitaine. Eleanor, who had insisted on maintaining the independence of the duchy, divorced Louis in 1152 and promptly married Henry Plantagenet, Count of Anjou, Duke of Normandy and future King of England. On his succession to the throne in 1154, Henry II proceeded to join much of western France to the English crown and in so doing set the scene for future conflict; after his death, however, Henry's great empire diminished rapidly, fuelled by inter-familial strife. Richard Coeur de Lion succeeded Henry in 1189 and continued – until he was killed at the siege of Châlus in 1199 – to assert his claim to Aquitaine. In the early thirteenth century King John of England was finally driven from France and Périgord once again fell into the hands of a French monarch, Philip Augustus. In 1259 the Treaty of Paris between Louis IX of France and Henry III of England returned most of the Plantagenet lands to England and divided the region, turning it into frontier territory. The intermittent nature of the warfare allowed castles to be built, churches to be fortified, and revolutionary fortified villages – the *bastides* – to be established. Built by both the French and the English, these *bastides* were inhabited by freemen.

Despite the turbulence in the Dordogne in the Middle Ages the population began to increase and the forest was slowly cleared for agricultural use, often under the direction and encouragement of the Church and the religious orders. Trade routes were kept open, essential for the rapidly expanding trade in wine. River traffic on the Dordogne was constant, with boats laden with wine from Bergerac destined for ports in both France and England.

An uneasy peace existed between the two opposing factions from the time of the Treaty of Paris until 1294, when Philip IV confiscated Gascony from the English. Years of fighting and treaty-making followed until, in 1337, Philip confiscated English territory yet again, deploying his army in the Garonne valley. Edward III retaliated by seizing French property in England and by declaring himself King of France. Thus ensued what has come to be known as the Hundred Years War. In fact, it lasted for more than a hundred years and was not so much a continuous war, rather a series of intermittent skirmishes, battles and sieges which devastated Périgord and left it with its great legacy of castles. The wine growers and merchants of Bordeaux were fearful that their valuable trade with England would be destroyed and appealed to Edward III for aid. Edward used this as a pretext to invade the whole region; he sent his son the Black Prince into Périgord where he laid waste the countryside. But the English armies were over-extended and the tide of war turned against them; by 1444 they had been forced from eastern Périgord and even Bordeaux – long held by the English – fell to the French in 1451. But the merchants of Bordeaux who had prospered under the English were opposed to change and when faced with higher taxes they rose against the French king. The legendary soldier Sir John Talbot, Earl of Shrewsbury, was sent to give support to the revolt of the Bordelais, but he met defeat and death at the Battle of Castillon. It was this battle, near Libourne on the Dordogne, which led to the English finally being expelled from the whole of France (except Calais), and to the end of the Hundred Years War.

Périgord was at last rid of the English but the years of constant warfare had taken their toll of the countryside and the local population. The war and internal political strife had led once again to large-scale depopulation in the region. Castles and their supporting village communities had been destroyed. Disease and famine added to the hardship; the Black Death had come to Périgord in 1348 reducing the population of prosperous Sarlat by half.

Tax incentives brought an influx of settlers to the region and a period of reconstruction and restoration of buildings ensued in an atmosphere of relative calm. No sooner it seemed had Périgord embarked on the road to economic recovery and population growth than it was once again plunged into another protracted period of bitter warfare. The Reformation of the sixteenth century, involving a revolt against the worldly state of the Catholic Church, was marked by a rise in allegiance to the more disciplined Protestant order. Succeeding monarchs, at first sympathetic to the Protestant cause, retreated into a state of entrenched orthodoxy. At the same time increasing numbers of the disaffected aristocracy and bourgeoisie pledged their allegiance to the newly-formed Protestant Huguenot party, as Protestantism, once wholly religious, became increasingly a political movement. The massacre of Vassy in 1562 sowed the seeds for the civil wars known as the Wars of Religion, which raged until 1598, when Henry of Navarre granted the Huguenots freedom of worship under the Edict of Nantes. During the war the Protestants had allied themselves with the kings of Navarre who supported their cause, and the wars were fought most intensely in the southwest where there was the strongest support for Henry of Navarre. These wars were particularly savage; towns and villages were repeatedly sacked and the destruction of ecclesiastical buildings was wholesale. Local loyalties were torn as neighbouring villages rallied to either the Catholic or the Protestant cause. Important towns like Bergerac and Sainte-Foy-la-Grande were champions of Protestantism while Périgueux remained a stronghold of the Catholic Holy League set up to combat the spread of Calvinism. The poor fared the worst as, enduring another outbreak of plague, they had to suffer as the armies plundered their holdings and lived off their land.

The Wars of Religion came officially to an end with the Edict of Nantes, but they had left the Dordogne not only with a trail of destruction but with a great feeling of discontent amongst the peasantry. In this region, where the landholders owned the great estates, the principal agricultural system was *métayage*, a form of sharecropping whereby the tenant farmer rented his land from the landowner for periods of one year at a time. The system was open to exploitation by unscrupulous landowners and, towards the end of the sixteenth century, the oppression by the gentry, combined with crippling taxation, engendered rebellion and peasant revolt. The first uprising of the so-called *croquants*, named after their favourite weapon, the *cros* (a bent pitchfork) came in 1594 and lasted off and on for three years. The nobility – Protestant and Catholic alike – were quick to realise their mutual interest in putting an end to the insurrection when their châteaux were burnt, so they formed a united force that swiftly crushed the peasant rebellion. Henry IV granted the peasantry tax concessions that went some way towards reducing the discontent, but in the 1630s punishing taxation was again introduced because of France's involvement in the costly Thirty Years War: the *croquants* were again up in arms, fighting battles at Monpazier and Eymet and at Bergerac, where an army of ten thousand men captured the town. This series of uprisings was brutally suppressed by the landowners and the *croquants'* formerly well-organized military campaign deteriorated into guerilla resistance that nevertheless lasted for several years.

Despite constant political upheaval and domestic strife during the latter half of the seventeenth century and the early part of the eighteenth, Périgord enjoyed a period of considerable economic growth. The revocation of the Edict of Nantes in 1685 had led to a mass exodus of the Huguenots, including in their number many skilled and enterprising members of the community. Inevitably this slowed the pace of progress and yet, by the mid-eighteenth century, Périgord was at the peak of its prosperity. This change in fortune was due to the expansion of the iron industry in the Nontronnais region, the exploitation of the region's forests for timber and paper-making, and the development of a more varied system of agriculture which survives to this day, involving the growth of speculative mixed crops. The wine trade had developed during the latter half of the seventeenth century with demand from the Dutch for white wine. Vine-growing underwent considerable expansion at this time, the region's rivers becoming like transport arteries.

The French Revolution of 1789 did not exactly revolutionize life in Périgord. Some of the land holdings of the Church and the nobility were certainly seized and put up for sale but, needless to say, the peasantry could not afford to buy them. What properties that did change hands were purchased by the urban bourgeoisie who then became integrated with the old order of aristocratic landowners, and the system of *métayage* persisted, although there was a movement towards increased ownership of land by peasant proprietors in the nineteenth century. Périgord became one of the new *départements* – at that time totalling eighty-three – and was renamed Dordogne. In accordance perhaps with the prevailing egalitarian spirit of the age it was decided that three towns would serve as capital of the *département* for a year at a time. Périgueux would start the sequence to be followed by Sarlat and Bergerac in turn. The plan was seemingly abandoned as unworkable on its inception and Périgueux has remained the capital ever since. By way of compensation Bergerac and Sarlat were created *sous-préfectures* together with Riberac and Nontron, each town controlling an *arrondissement* corresponding with the respective regional river basins, reflecting the four tribal divisions of ancient Périgord.

CHÂTEAU DE HAUTEFORT

The Château de Hautefort stands on the site of a twelfth-century building, once the home of the celebrated troubadour Bertrand de Born, whose political intrigues led to his immortalization in Dante's *Inferno*. The present château was built between 1644 and 1680 for Jacques-François de Hautefort. Its imposing mass overlooks a broad expanse of heath and woodland, and dominates the village below. Well-kept gardens planted with boxwood knots spread along the terraces beneath the great round towers, which are domed and topped with lantern turrets. Since 1929 the château has been owned by the Bastard family and in 1968 it narrowly escaped complete destruction when a devastating fire reduced it to little more than a roofless shell. Some of the furniture and tapestries were saved and careful restoration has replaced much of the fine interior. It is open to the public and includes a museum devoted to the novelist Eugène le Roy, who was born here.

The population of the Dordogne increased rapidly in the first half of the nineteenth century, largely because of the improvement in agricultural practice. New crops such as tobacco were cultivated, and crop rotation was introduced, which improved and made more use of the land. Great tracts of forest were cleared and put under vines, and by the mid-nineteenth century wine was by far the largest single product of the *département*. The labour-intensive nature of vine growing and the production of wine called for a corresponding increase in the population in those areas where vines were the major crop.

The era of agricultural prosperity came to an end in the 1880s when the vineyards were all but completely destroyed by phylloxera, an aphid pest that destroys the roots of the vine; only the wine-producing area around Bergerac survived the crisis. Between 1886 and 1921 three quarters of the population left the land to look for work in the towns. This rural exodus coincided with a downturn in local industry, which was aggravated by the advent of the railway; new products were brought to the region making many of the craft industries unviable, and cheaply produced iron was introduced too, which led to a decline in the region's iron industry. The local towns could not support the movement of people from the land and many peasants and rural craftsmen left to find work in the manufacturing centres, or emigrated, many going to Latin America.

The phylloxera crisis had proved catastrophic for the region. Vineyards were destroyed, never to be replanted, and whole farms were sold off or, in many cases, simply abandoned to become overgrown, their buildings left to fall derelict. The system of *métayage* had more or less broken down and the comparatively few farmers who did remain fell back upon subsistence polyculture, producing *'un peu de tout'* (a little of everything), a tradition of farming still very much in evidence in the Dordogne today. Those leaving the land at this time were predominantly the young and the effects of depopulation were further exacerbated by the First World War, in which forty thousand men from the Dordogne perished. The birth rate of the region fell to such an extent that between the wars the number of deaths had begun to outweigh the number of births. Any attempt at agricultural reform was severely hindered by the lack of enterprising young people, the almost deserted countryside being farmed by an increasingly elderly population. In the 1920s Breton farmers were encouraged to come to the region in order not only to ease the increasing overpopulation in Brittany but also to swell the dwindling population of the Dordogne. In all some ten thousand Breton farmers settled in the region.

An easing in the controls on the growing of tobacco has allowed the agricultural economy to pick up again, the Dordogne now being the second largest tobacco-producing *département*. Farming practice has kept abreast of the times; there has been an increase in mechanization and some rationalization of the small land-holdings; new crops have been introduced; and modern farming methods implemented. Nevertheless the rewards from the land are hard won and the young continue to leave the countryside to earn a living in the towns. The present-day population of the *département* is under four hundred thousand, little more than in Roman times.

The continuing depopulation of the countryside has meant that many of the region's cottages and farmhouses have become *maisons secondaires*, holiday homes for French families from Bordeaux, or from as far away as Paris, and for an increasing number of foreigners too, predominantly the English, to whom the lush greenness of the landscape may seem reassuringly familiar whilst having the added bonus of dependably hot summers. The work of restoring run-down properties for use as second homes has provided much-needed employment for the area's artisans and craftsmen, and the marked increase of tourism in the region has brought prosperity with it, especially for the hoteliers, restaurateurs and shopkeepers.

There is much to attract the visitor to the Dordogne: its castles and caves, its many fêtes, the river itself and the delights of the regional cuisine. But what draws most people back a second or third time is the sheer beauty of its scenery, in which man has made his presence felt in a most harmonious way. Forty years ago Philip Oyler, in his book *The Generous Earth*, expressed what may still be experienced today:

'At my feet the limestone, which underlies this whole region, ended with a perpendicular cliff of one thousand feet, and I looked out over the Dordogne valley, a mile or more across, to seemingly endless hills beyond, with the wide clear river, still in places and with the mirrored spires of poplars in it, forming islands and small cascades in others. In the valley I could see countless little homesteads, innumerable plots of cultivation. Near the river itself and on the slopes adjoining were lush-looking pastures. Up the steeper slopes were vineyards, above them woods, which reached right up to the top of the hills, wherever the sides were not too steep for a tree to find a footing.

'It was a panorama that spelt wealth to me, true wealth. All was bounty and beauty, God-given, and man had not desecrated it. He had substituted his crops and fruit trees for wild flowers and bushes, he had utilized the river to drive his water-mills, he had

NEAR SERVANCHES

There are now about a hundred small *étangs* (lakes) in the Double but once there were many more. In the nineteenth century many were drained in an attempt to combat the malaria endemic to the region. Some of the lakes are man-made, created in the Middle Ages to provide a source of fish for the villagers and, more importantly, for the monastic orders, like the Carthusian brethren at nearby Vauclaire. Once every few years the villagers would completely drain one of the *étangs*, collect the fish lying on the bottom and take them to market in baskets lined with straw. This was a common practice, especially around Easter when demand for fish was high, and it was an occasion for much merriment and celebration. Today the *étangs* are still a valuable source of fish, but some of the larger ones like the Étang de la Jemaye have been developed for water sports and recreation.

felled trees from time immemorial according as he needed them and filled up the gap with seedlings. He had in fact been wise enough to make return for aught that he had taken. If anyone should desire earnestly to know how this earth of ours can be used to serve all the needs of man without being spoilt, he can go and see for himself.'

The *département* of the Dordogne is loosely subdivided into a number of regions, whose names are derived from the principal towns (like 'Bergeracois'), the forests (like the 'Double'), or, in recent years, the ingenuity of the tourist board (like 'Périgord Vert'). The names of the various regions may seem fanciful at first but they are a reflection of the real physical variation in the *département* which exhibits immense diversity, ranging from the *pechs*, the densely wooded hills of the west, to the *causses*, the arid limestone plateaux of the east. The demarcation between these regions is not strict, the boundaries may shift and overlap and the question of whether a particular town or village is located in one region or another may be the subject of some gentle dispute, but as a rule the system is both workable and convenient.

In order to impose a structure on a region of such diversity and variety we have simply divided the *département* into two: Périgueux and the North and the Dordogne valley and the South. In each section we start in the west and move progressively eastwards, keeping within the boundaries of the *département* except where we have followed the river Dordogne upstream as far as Beaulieu-sur-Dordogne in the *département* of Corrèze. Between the departmental border and Beaulieu are to be found many places of interest and great beauty, which beg to be included and which form a natural part of what visitors to the Dordogne region might include on their itinerary.

Different sources use different spellings for many of the place names in the Dordogne. For uniformity we have taken the spelling of almost all place names from the excellent Michelin maps of the area.

PÉRIGUEUX AND THE NORTH

BOURDEILLES

The delightful town of Bourdeilles, ten kilometres south of Brantôme, spreads over both banks of the Dronne. A beautiful Gothic bridge that incorporates passing places for packhorses spans the river. The town is dominated by its château, which stands atop a limestone cliff that rises above the river. Gérard de Maumont built the château between 1283 and 1298 on the foundations of a fortress dating from when Bourdeilles was created one of the four great baronies of Périgord. The château is largely in ruins but its impressive octagonal machicolated keep is still complete, forty metres high, with walls more than two metres thick. Beside these medieval ruins stands a Renaissance château, built by Jacquette de Montbron, chatelaine of Bourdeilles and sister-in-law of the soldier and historian Brantôme, who was born here.

At the heart of the Dordogne *département* on the Isle stands its capital, the bustling market town of Périgueux, once the capital of ancient Périgord and now the administrative, industrial and commercial centre of the Dordogne, where all roads meet. The region surrounding the town is nowadays referred to as Périgord Central and covers a large area roughly delimited by Brantôme to the north and Lalinde to the south, Neuvic-sur-l'Isle to the west and Thenon to the east. To the west of Périgord Central, lying between the valleys of the Dronne and the Isle is the region known as the Double. This is a somewhat desolate area of low hills and ridges and of dark forests of oak, chestnut and maritime pine, sparsely populated and dotted with numerous small lakes, natural and man-made. The Chevalier de Lagrange-Chancel, writing in the eighteenth century, described the Double as *'un pays affreux'* (a frightful country); this was a feeling apparently supported by the peasants to whom it was *'le pays nègre'* (the black country) – a region inhabited by wolves, snakes and wild boar, and frequented by horse thieves. Life here for the peasant population was disease-ridden and poverty-stricken; Eugene Le Roy immortalized it at the turn of the century in his novel *L'Enemi de la Mort*. Sixty per cent of the Double is still under forest but today there are thriving dairy farms in the well-cultivated valleys and the many areas of unspoilt natural beauty, the gentle rivers Dronne and Isle and the lakes and pools – some developed for fishing and water sports – are a great attraction for visitors in the summer months. The principal towns in the region are Montpon-Ménestérol, once renowned for its roses; Mussidan, a small industrial town specializing in ceramics; and Neuvic-sur-l'Isle with its splendid château, an important centre of the region's flourishing footwear industry.

Moving eastwards from the Double one enters the region known as the Ribéracois. This area is less forested than the Double and the frequent outcrops of chalky limestone that impart a whitish hue to the landscape lend it its alternative name of Périgord Blanc. Ribérac, on the Dronne, formerly a sub-prefecture of the Dordogne, is the most important town in the region with a population of around four thousand. A market is held there every Friday and a basket and wickerwork fair every Wednesday from May until September. As an important agricultural centre for the region it plays host to a great agricultural fair in August as well as catering for the tourist influx, who come to enjoy the excellent walks and pretty unspoilt villages that the area has to offer.

Between Ribérac and Brantôme the river Dronne runs through what is undisputedly one of the most beautiful valleys in France. Up until the nineteenth century the river passed through gently rolling hills clad with vines but the phylloxera crisis put paid to the once prosperous vineyards and for its livelihood today the region depends upon cereals and livestock – for dairy produce and for veal.

Beyond Brantôme to the north lies the busy town of Nontron, beautifully situated between two ravines, with a splendid view over the river Bandiat. The town lends its name to the region, the Nontronnais, that has relatively recently come to be known as Périgord Vert because of the lush greenness of its well-watered pasture and woodland. Below the hills that border the Limousin is a plateau, deeply fissured by the valleys of several rivers – the Isle, Dronne, Loue, Côle, Auvézère and Bandiat. The swiftly flowing Bandiat once provided the source of power for small steel works and sawmills but today those industries, together with the milling of grain, have gone, to be replaced, mainly by tourism. Having as it does a high rainfall, the climate of the Nontronnais is damp, and the land is not given to arable farming. Instead it resembles the Limousin with large expanses of chestnut woods and lush green pasture interspersed with tracts of moorland covered with gorse and heather. Isolated farms are engaged in the production of meat and dairy produce; agriculture and tourism have largely superseded the timber industry and its offshoots such as cabinet-making and cooperage for the wine trade, which once formed the basis of the region's economy.

Heading towards the eastern edge of the *département* the terrain and the pattern of agriculture change. And as one moves south towards the lowland region around Hautefort the climate becomes warmer and drier than that of the plateaux to the north and south. In this intensively farmed area the climate and the soil are suitable for growing tobacco, cherries and vines, and above all walnuts which have greatly added to the rural economy. Paper-making once thrived in the valley of the Isle near Thiviers, where the river provided lime-free water and an abundance of power sites for driving the watermills, and iron foundries like that at La Forge d'Ans proliferated

VILLEFRANCHE-DE-LONCHAT

Here, in late spring, the vines show the first flush of the new season's growth, springing from the dead-looking cutback stool of the previous year. The vines have escaped the frosts and will receive constant attention until the *vendange* (the grape harvest) in the autumn.

along the fast-flowing Auvézère, the furnaces being supplied with local ore and char-coal. None of this industry has survived and the economy of the region is now founded on the flourishing agriculture and on market gardening.

Périgueux, steeped in history, is an obvious attraction to the tourist with its Gallo-Roman remains, its great Cathedral of Saint-Front and the well-restored buildings of its old town, but the whole of the *département* to the north is a most rewarding area to explore possessing as it does such an immense diversity of landscape and architecture. The compact towns of Brantôme and Bourdeilles, both situated on a peaceful stretch of the beautiful Dronne within a few miles of each other, possess superb Renaissance and medieval buildings. Romanesque churches, often fortified around the time of the Hundred Years War, are found throughout the region, with fine examples at Saint-Privat-des-Prés and at Grand-Brassac, where the church is decorated with an unusual collection of early sculpture. The countryside is liberally dotted with great châteaux dating from the Middle Ages and the Renaissance: the Château de Puyguilhem at Villars and the Château de Tinteillac near Chapdeuil, to name but two. Apart from the churches there are the remains of other great medieval religious buildings to visit and admire: the beautifully restored Augustinian abbey of Chancelade – part Romanesque, part seventeenth-century – and, hidden in the forest near Périgueux, the lovely remains of the priory of Merlande.

The vernacular architecture, in contrast to the great châteaux, churches and abbeys, is of much more modest proportions, but is no less of a delight. Farm buildings, sometimes complete with their great *greniers*, are built on strictly functional lines yet they remain perfectly pleasing to the eye, constructed as they are of local materials, stone or half-timbered, and roofed in the warm brown tiles or limestone *lauzes* characteristic of the *département*, so that they blend harmoniously with the landscape. The agricultural system of polyculture, practised widely throughout the region, is another source of great beauty, small parcels of mixed crops such as tobacco, vines, strawberries or maize being juxtaposed with small groves of poplars, fruit trees, walnuts and chestnuts and pasture for livestock.

NEAR AUBETERRE

Avenues of plane trees are a
common sight all over France;
they are said to have been
planted on the orders of
Napoleon Bonaparte to give
shade to marching troops.
Regular lopping of the lower
branches allows traffic to pass
by unimpeded, while also
encouraging the growth of a
thick leafy canopy in the
summer months. These fine
trees, with their decorative
border of wild flowers, line the
road leading to Aubeterre.

THE DRONNE AT CHENAUD

Here, next to a large farm situated opposite the village of Chenaud, the Dronne flows over one of the largest weirs on the river, providing a popular spot for fishing. In total contrast to the austere plateaux of the region, the river valleys of the Dordogne have always been a centre of civilization, where men and women have lived for centuries cultivating the land and building manors, châteaux and farms.

LA LATIÈRE, NEAR
SAINT-AULAYE

The inhospitable Double lies between the rivers Dronne and Isle, bounded to the east by the road from Ribérac to Mussidan. It is the wildest and least populated region in the Dordogne. Because of its poor soils and large areas of forest, only a poor living could be had from the land. Twice a year, when horse fairs were held, the population would be temporarily swelled. These fairs still happen near St-Aulaye on the edge of the forest at La Latière. Once the resort of horse thieves, La Latière was on the pilgrim route to Santiago de Compostela and pilgrims and gypsies alike would assemble here to buy and sell horses. Today the livestock has changed. Forest clearance and improvement in drainage have allowed for the raising of cattle, and the Double now competes with the Ribéracois to the north in the production of veal and dairy produce.

The first fair of the year is held on 1 May and as the mist of early morning lifts, trading begins. Hundreds of young geese are on sale and they will be bought for fattening – outdoors at first and then inside, when they are force fed to produce the *foie gras* much in demand by gourmets. At midday those attending the fair will fatten themselves at the *plein air* lunch which all are invited to partake, under the appreciative gaze of the prime Charollais cattle.

GAMANSON

These ancient dwellings at
Gamanson, on the southern
fringe of the Double, near the
industrial town of Mussidan
on the Isle, are reaching the
end of their useful life. In
many ways they are typical of
Périgord, their steeply pitched
roofs taking on a gentler angle
near the base where round tiles
may be used. Because they
have no gutters, the eaves
project well beyond the walls,
to protect them from rain.
Lucarnes (dormer windows)
light the roof space and the
little triangular openings,
outeaux, provide ventilation.
Buildings are generally
constructed of materials
available within the vicinity,
and stone is usually found
nearby. But it is scarce in the
Double and these houses are
timber-framed, with an infill
of wattle and daub. It seems
unlikely that they will ever be
inhabited again as convoluted
inheritance laws impede the
sale of property and the Double
is an area still undergoing
depopulation.

NEAR ECHOURGNAC

Wood has provided an income
for the villagers of the Double
for centuries. The most
common tree is the oak, both
the white oak, which gives
timber that can be used in
carpentry, and the black oak,
used for fuel and charcoal.
Maritime pine became
established in the nineteenth
century to aid drainage and
provide resin for making
turpentine. Woodland is now
being cleared in the Double for
the cultivation of strawberries,
which thrive on the relatively
poor soil. Echourgnac, in the
heart of the Double, was once
malaria-ridden, but in the
nineteenth century a Trappist
monastery was founded here,
the Trappe de Bonne
Espérance, and the monks
proceeded to drain the marshy
land and raise cattle. The
Trappists are still there, and
they produce their own cheese,
La Trappe, that can be bought
at the monastery gates.

NEAR CUMOND

Maize has been grown in the region since the seventeenth century, principally as fodder for livestock, especially pigs and geese. Since World War II the availability of better-yielding hybrid varieties has led to an increase in the popularity of maize as a crop. Often improvising with an old high-sided cart, many farms have erected makeshift silos of wood and wire netting, where the maize is kept outside for use throughout the winter. Boiled maize is force-fed to geese in the production of *foie-gras* and yellow-skinned maize-fed chickens are becoming more common in shops and markets. Occasionally maize is also used for domestic cookery; it is ground and mixed with wheat flour, eggs and lard, making dumplings called *miques*, which are eaten with a meat stew. The *cocoricots*, the cobs stripped of their grain, are used as domestic fuel in winter.

SAINT-PRIVAT-DES-PRÉS

Lying in the midst of acres of rolling agricultural land, the little village of Saint-Privat-des-Prés is dominated by its massive fortified church, one of the most perfect domed Romanesque churches in Périgord. The church is rather low and box-like without a belfry, but the rows of blind arcading along the exterior walls serve to relieve this sober effect and give character to the church. The west façade is in the Saintonge style, with an upper row of blind arcades and an immense cavernous doorway beneath a row of nine recessed blind arches. Inside, the barrel-vaulted nave is spanned by arches that rest on columns topped by finely carved capitals. The cartulary of St Saure, which gives the titles to the estates and monasteries of the region, records the church as being a Benedictine priory in 1108. The church was probably fortified against the threat of attack because of its proximity to the borders of the old provinces of Guyenne and Angoumois.

LUSIGNAC

Northwest of Ribérac, the village of Lusignac looks out across the open farmland of the Ribéracois. This region is often referred to as Périgord Blanc because of the chalky limestone content of the soil – most noticeable in the spring when the fields are freshly ploughed and harrowed. The buildings, of greyish-white local stone, add to the overall effect of whiteness in the landscape. A splash of colour is imparted by the roofs, which are covered with a mixture of flat and rounded tiles, the hand-made *tuiles-canals*, Roman tiles, which are easy to make and cheap to lay. The château dates from the fourteenth century with later additions. Its high perimeter wall is broken by towers and fortified gatehouses. The area it encloses, the former fortress complex, is about the same size as the remainder of the village.

The church too is fortified. Built in the twelfth century, severe and unornamented, it has a massive machicolated bell tower, furnished with arrow slits and capped with a shallow-pitched roof. The interior is plain and unremarkable, with a somewhat damaged sixteenth-century *pietà* and a seventeenth-century carved wooden retable.

CHÂTEAU DE TINTEILLAC, NEAR CHAPDEUIL

Between Chapdeuil and Bourg-des-Maisons stands the Château de Tinteillac. Its twin fortified towers roofed with slate appear to stand guard over the Renaissance domestic quarters. Farm buildings and dovecots – once the privilege of only the very wealthy – cluster around the château, and the courtyard, with its broad sweep of drive, is enclosed by a crenellated wall with arched gateways. This quite modest seigneurial manor house is at the heart of a working farm and as such has an air of elegance without appearing in any way pretentious. Nearby Chapdeuil is a small town of attractive old houses; it is dominated by a moated château with a massive keep and fifteenth-century battlements.

TOCANE-SAINT-APRE

The charming little town of Tocane-Saint-Apre on the Dronne is the agricultural centre of the valley. The classical eighteenth-century Château de Fayolle, just south of the town, was the home of the Marquis de Fayolle, the agricultural theorist who, in the early nineteenth century, was an advocate for the improvement both of current agricultural practice and of the rights of the *métayers* (tenant farmers). He was greatly in favour of mechanization both to increase yields for the proprietor and to ease the labour of the *métayer*. The almost feudal system of *métayage* had operated since the sixteenth century and it survived virtually unchanged until 1946. The landowner rented his land on a yearly basis and supplied seed, agricultural implements and cattle for the tenant's use, but in return he was to receive half the produce from the tenant's holding.

NEAR CELLES

Few farms in the Dordogne are without at least one walnut tree and here the farmer has planted a small stand in an arable field currently under cereal. The *département* is the leading producer of walnuts in France. The climate is well suited for their cultivation, with its wet springs and its summers with occasional rain, followed by late hot spells; there is also an abundance of suitable soil like clay or limestone. Recognized as an economic asset for centuries, the trees provided not only a source of food but also a cash crop, and the oil extracted from them could be used for cooking and lighting the home. At the end of its productive life the tree would yield its timber, once much in demand for furniture and for veneers used in cabinet-making. Harvesting is still done by hand; so is walnut cracking, a task largely performed by the village women in the winter months.

PAUSSAC-ET-SAINT-VIVIEN

The domed Romanesque church at Paussac-et-Saint-Vivien, just north of Bourdeilles, possesses delicately ornamented blind arcades along its south side, and the capitals both inside and out are finely carved with human faces and birds. The intricacy of the decoration is rather overwhelmed by the incongruous fortification added in the fifteenth century. Nearby can be seen the dolmen de Peyrelevade and the dolmen de Peyre d'Ermale, massive solitary standing stones that once were part of Neolithic burial chambers. Until last century many more of these dolmens and stone circles existed. Many were demolished and the stones taken either as building material or, with the increase in iron foundries, to provide bases for anvils and presses.

GRAND-BRASSAC

The little village of Grand-Brassac lies to the north of Montagrier and the green valley of the Dronne. The formidable Romanesque church was built in the twelfth century on a modest scale with a single dome. In the thirteenth century it was given two additional domes and was heavily fortified so that it might act as a refuge; its defensive galleries, battlements and loopholes give it more the appearance of a fortress than a church. During the Wars of Religion the church was greatly damaged by the Protestants, but it was later repaired and given a new apse by Antoine de Montagrier at the end of the sixteenth century. The interior is surprisingly small. The sixteenth-century vaulted choir blends harmoniously with the earlier structure, while the overall impression of height is emphasized by the narrow nave.

Perhaps in an attempt to soften the austere, martial aspect of the church's exterior, the north doorway is decorated with a remarkable assemblage of sculpture from different periods. At the centre of the group is a Romanesque portal, its archway carved with fanciful beasts and stylized leaves. Within the arch is a group of statuettes, still bearing traces of their original polychrome decoration, which depict the Adoration of the Magi. Above the arch sits a sixteenth-century carving of Christ in Majesty between the Virgin and St John, with the figures of St Peter and St Paul below. The collection of sculptures, spanning four centuries, blend perfectly to form a charming, cohesive whole.

RIVER DRONNE AT BOURDEILLES

The Dronne runs swiftly below the twin châteaux on the cliff, providing motive power for the restored seventeenth-century water mill – built like a ship below the ramparts. Having driven the mill wheel, the river rushes over a weir and under the medieval bridge to spread forth more calmly, shallow enough in spring and summer to allow mid-stream fishing in its clean green waters.

NEAR CHAMPAGNAC-DE-BELAIR

Farm buildings were constructed of readily available local materials and built to stand the test of time. This seventeenth-century stone-built barn, with its *grenier* (loft) for storage of hay or grain accessible only by ladder, is as functional now as the day it was first put into service. It stands just outside the beautifully named little town of Champagnac-de-Belair on the Dronne, which relies upon agriculture for its existence. An important market is held here on the first Monday of the month and a sheep fair once a year. Walnuts are grown locally and walnut oil is still produced, although the old walnut-oil mill, Moulin du Roc, has now been converted into a restaurant with a fine reputation for its superb cuisine.

BRANTÔME

The small medieval and Renaissance town of Brantôme sits on an island where the Dronne briefly divides, and hence is dubbed 'the Venice of Périgord'. The town grew up around the Benedictine abbey reputedly founded by Charlemagne in 769. It was to this abbey that he gave the relics of St Sicaire, one of the Holy Innocents murdered by King Herod. Sacked by the Normans in 849 and rebuilt in the eleventh century, the abbey was subsequently radically altered on several occasions; in the nineteenth-century the abbey church and buildings were finally restored by the architect Abadie. The oldest surviving building is the eleventh-century belfry. Built apart from the church, it is the finest Romanesque belfry in Périgord. The abbatial buildings are now used for municipal purposes and as a museum.

Many of the Renaissance and older houses have gardens that overlook the river. The monastic garden, which contains a delightful Renaissance pavilion, may be reached by crossing an elbow bridge over the Dronne. Here the town's most famous commendatory abbot, Pierre de Bourdeilles, known as Brantôme, wrote his sensational *Dames Galantes*, a risqué portrait of sixteenth-century court life. Brantôme's early career was as a soldier of fortune fighting not only in France but also on campaigns in Italy, Spain and Africa. He accompanied Mary Queen of Scots as a courtier on her return to Scotland. But his military and court life came to an end when he was crippled by a fall from his horse. He returned to the abbey at Brantôme to write; the chronicles of court life he produced, however, were only published posthumously.

CONDAT-SUR-TRINCOU

Condat is the Celtic word for confluence; Condat-sur-Trincou, just south of Champagnac-de-Belair, is a pretty village perched on a rocky cliff above the rivers Côle and Trincou. The heavily fortified Romanesque church, with its extravagant belltower and powerful buttresses, was built on the site of a Gallo-Roman necropolis where hundreds of sarcophagi were discovered. A triple-headed statue of Hercules was found there in 1800, which can now be seen in the museum at Bordeaux. North of the church are the remains of the defensive ramparts that once encircled the village. From La Chapelle-Faucher, just south of the village, a spectacular view can be gained of a château; set high above a river, it is a scene typical of the Dordogne region. The fifteenth-century château, partly destroyed by fire having been struck by lightning, has two massive crenellated towers that are still inhabited.

CHÂTEAU DE PUYGUILHEM, NEAR VILLARS

A carriage road lined with huge lime trees leads to the magnificent Château de Puyguilhem on a hillside near Villars. Construction of the château was started in the early sixteenth century by Mondot de la Marthonie, first president of the *parlements* of Paris and Bordeaux. When Mondot died at Blois in 1517, possibly from poisoning, the work was taken over by his son Geoffroy, and was completed in 1530. Stylistically the château bears more than a passing resemblance to some of the great Renaissance châteaux of the Loire, built in the reign of François I; but much of the ornate sculpture and carved decoration both inside and out was probably carried out by local craftsmen. Sacked during the Revolution, the château was allowed to fall into woeful disrepair until it was bought by the State – with supreme foresight – in 1939 and restored by the Beaux-Arts, its empty rooms once again being filled with furniture.

SAINT-JEAN-DE-CÔLE

This near-perfect village east of Villars has a splendid roofscape that in the past has won for it a national 'best roof award'. The medieval houses are built of golden stone or half-timbered; their walls are bowed by age, and they are roofed with flat and round lichen-covered tiles. They cluster around the huge market square and the curious twelfth-century church, next to a Gothic hump-backed bridge which spans the river Côle.

The church, the chapel of a former priory, was built without a nave but with a vast choir and apsidal chapels. It once possessed a huge dome twelve metres in diameter, but it was poorly supported and collapsed in 1787 and again in 1860 having been rebuilt. The citizens then conceded defeat and constructed a wooden ceiling to fill the space. Nevertheless, the church is still beautiful; it has a fine belfry and much interesting sculpture. Sadly, all that remains of the conventual buildings is part of the sixteenth-century cloister. But across the broad square from the covered market hall three half-timbered, gabled houses have been converted into a museum of local arts and crafts, with displays describing the daily lives of the blacksmiths, farmers and vine growers of earlier times.

NONTRON

Nontron is the principal town of the Nontronnais, an area of lush pasture and chestnut forest, north of Périgueux. The market town stands picturesquely on a promontory between two ravines, with the valley of the river Bandiat below. The impressive ramparts of the medieval château still stand, but the château itself was totally destroyed during the Wars of Religion and rebuilt in the eighteenth century. The fast-flowing Bandiat once provided the waterpower for grain- and saw-milling, and for the manufacturing industries. In the nineteenth century Nontron was the commercial centre for the region's iron and steel industry. It was renowned for the manufacture of the pocket knives with boxwood handles that are still produced in a small way here today, although the town's economy now relies on tourism and the footwear industry.

SAINT-MARTIN-LE-PIN

The charming village of Saint-Martin-le-Pin lies six kilometres northwest of Nontron and possesses an unpretentious rustic Romanesque church with a fine twelfth-century south door. Much of the original carving around the portal has survived and the lively detail is well preserved, yet its precise significance is lost to us. Familiar wild and domestic beasts cavort with a fanciful dragon with a twisting tail; and human figures are seen carrying milk pails and sheaves of corn, blowing hunting horns or being pursued by demons – a reminder for the twelfth-century churchgoer of his own mortality and of the perils of falling into sin. The interior of the church is plain and undecorated, harmonious and well proportioned, with a rounded apse described by the French as *cul-de-four*, which means literally 'oven-vaulted'.

VILLEFRANCHE-DE-LONCHAT

Just inside the western boundary of the *département*, and occupying a fine hilltop site, is the town of Villefranche-de-Lonchat, built as a *bastide* for Edward III in 1287. The regular grid pattern of its streets is still in evidence but little else that makes it recognizable as a *bastide*. Several medieval towns go under the name of Villefranche, literally meaning 'free town'. The villagers were freed from the feudal manorial duties when they agreed to build and populate the bastides, being given a house and a plot of land of their own in return. The slopes surrounding the town are clad with serried rows of vines, for this is wine producing country. Villefranche lies just over the border from Saint-Emilion and the fine-wine producers of the Bordelais, whose reputation somewhat overshadows the very decent *vins du pays* produced in Périgord.

CHÂTEAU DE MATECOULON, MONTPEYROUX

Montpeyroux occupies a hilltop site on the western edge of the Dordogne, with fine south views over rolling hills to the valley of the Lidoire below. The twelfth-century church, domed and 'oven-vaulted', has an elegant apse in the Saintonge style and ornamented blind arcading. There is much high-quality carving, with nearly a hundred carved heads around the cornice. Side by side with the church, in the shade of its splendid old trees, stands the U-shaped Château de Matecoulon, solid and unpretentious, built in the seventeenth and eighteenth centuries. Its pepperpot tower, roofed in weathered tiles, serves also as *pigeonnier*, the three openings giving access to the pigeon loft above.

CHÂTEAU DE GURSON, NEAR CARSAC-DE-GURSON

Just east of Villefranche-de-Lonchat, high on a hill surrounded by woods and vineyards, the Château de Gurson stands in ruins. The original château was destroyed in 1254 and in 1277 Henry III gave the land to Jean de Grailly, Edward I's first seneschal of the Agenais and the creator of several bastides. Rebuilt in the fourteenth century, the château was badly damaged in the Hundred Years War and almost entirely rebuilt yet again in the eighteenth century. Montaigne, who lived nearby at Saint-Michel-de-Montaigne, was a frequent visitor here, and he wrote his famous essay on the education of children for the chatelaine of Gurson. The quiet hillside village of Carsac-de-Gurson has a well-preserved Romanesque church; it has a massive arcaded tower and a fine façade in the Saintonge style.

MONT-RÉAL, NEAR ISSAC

Issac stands on the river Crempse, southeast of the industrial town of Mussidan. From a rocky hilltop above the Crempse the Château de Mont-Réal dominates the old route between Mussidan and Bergerac. The château is a largely late-Renaissance building, set on earlier foundations and surrounded by the remains of eleventh-century ramparts. The beautiful sixteenth-century chapel was built by François de Pontbriand. It contains his tomb and that of one of his three wives, as well as the holy thorn carried by Sir John Talbot at the Battle of Castillon, where he met his untimely death. Legend has it that Montreal on the St Lawrence in Canada was so named by Claude de Pontbriand – a descendant of François, from Mont-Réal – who accompanied Jacques Cartier on his second visit to the New World.

NEAR LES LÈCHES

Using oxen to work the land is now a rare sight in the Dordogne, but until comparatively recently they were the most common form of motive power. Many farms, even if they do not have oxen, still have ox-carts tucked away in their outbuildings. Oxen are ideal draught animals for agricultural work, preferable in many ways to horses. They require a less costly diet than horses and they can work heavy soil and steep or irregular ground that would defeat a horse. They are docile and tractable, and a pair of oxen will plough as much in a day as a pair of horses – around half an acre. A few diehard enthusiasts are keeping the tradition alive and it is possible that, with the increase in organic farming, the use of oxen may enjoy a revival in the future.

NEAR NEUVIC-SUR-L'ISLE

Late September and the *vendange* (grape harvest) is well under way. Most small farmers keep at least a few rows of vines, enough to provide a supply of wine for home consumption; here the results of a bountiful summer are undergoing the first stage of their transformation into wine. The barrel-loads of grapes – white and black – are fed slowly into the hopper to be pressed. The hand-driven rollers are so constructed that, in expressing the juice, they crush only the flesh of the grapes and not the pips, which would impart a bitter flavour to the finished wine. With the year's bumper crop safely harvested the farmer-turned-*vigneron* can afford to smile in the pleasant anticipation of a well-stocked cellar.

CHÂTEAU DE NEUVIC-SUR-L'ISLE

Southwest of Périgueux, the small town of Neuvic-sur-l'Isle – a centre for the footwear industry – possesses this fine Renaissance château. The original château on this site was owned in the Middle Ages by the Talleyrand family, who sold it to the Marquis de Fayolle. It was rebuilt between 1520 and 1530 by his son, Annet, and has survived virtually unchanged. The turrets and machicolations attempt to give an impression of fortification but in fact they are merely decorative, adding interest to what would otherwise be rather a stark building – with mullioned windows and plain, unshuttered dormers. The château, standing in parkland close to the river, now serves as a school.

NEAR MANZAC

This splendid downland hillscape in the fertile valley of the river Vern gives one an idea of the system of mixed farming, polyculture, practised throughout the Dordogne. Many farms keep a small herd of cattle – Charollais, Limousin or other breeds – for both meat and dairy produce. Although the rich pasture is ideal for them, they will also graze the steep hillsides that are unsuitable for arable farming. The ploughed fields will probably be planted with tobacco or maize and the cereal field beyond is dotted with a few walnut trees, which will provide a little welcome extra income later in the year. Clumps of parasitic evergreen mistletoe can be seen growing high in the poplars in the foreground.

MERLANDE

The priory of Merlande, in a clearing deep in the heart of the Forêt de Feytaud, was founded by the monks of Chancelade, which lies eight kilometres away to the southeast towards Périgueux. Its remote location, close to a spring, made it an ideal site for those seeking both to lead a contemplative life and find an isolated refuge away from society, yet its history is anything but peaceful. Founded in 1142, all that remains of the former priory are the church and the prior's house.

The restored priory church once had two domes, but one was destroyed by the English in 1170 and replaced with broken-barrel vaulting. The church was fortified during the Wars of Religion, and indeed the defensive outworks can still be seen, but it suffered more damage at the hands of the Huguenots, and finally, during the Revolution, it was completely ransacked. In the nineteenth century it was the subject of a demolition order; fortunately this was rescinded, but only after the belfry had been dismantled. Inside, the twelfth-century capitals in the chancel are carved with a remarkable menagerie of fantastic beasts, and lions devouring palm-leaf scrolls. The prior's house, meanwhile, has been heavily restored and is now a private residence.

CHANCELADE

The abbey of Chancelade, six kilometres northwest of Périgueux, was founded by a monk from Charente in 1129 and later occupied by Augustinian canons. Once a large complex of buildings, the abbey suffered during the Hundred Years War and the Wars of Religion, but the much-restored church and some of the abbatial buildings have survived. Only the lower walls of the church with their blind arcading are Romanesque, the five-bay nave having been re-roofed in the seventeenth century with ogee vaulting. In the chancel there are fine seventeenth-century carved choir stalls and two fourteenth-century frescoes, which depict St Christopher and St Thomas Becket. The tiny Romanesque chapel of St Jean – on the other side of the square – once served the abbey.

PÉRIGUEUX

The four Celtic clans, the Petro-corii, gave their name both to Périgord and its capital Périgueux. It was here, on the south bank of the Isle, that they established their settlement that served as their territorial headquarters. The Petro-corii were unwilling to submit to Roman rule at first, but the town – then called Vesunna – prospered greatly and became one of the finest towns in Aquitaine, with temples, aqueducts and an amphitheatre that would seat thirty thousand. In the third century, heralding a period of decline for the town, the town was sacked by the Alemans. The Roman buildings were torn down to build defensive ramparts and the town, suffering successive barbarian onslaughts, withdrew into itself to become an almost anonymous enclave, until its fortunes were revived with the advent of St Front.

PÉRIGUEUX

The great Cathedral of St Front is built on the site of the tomb of the saint who, legend has it, converted Périgord to Christianity and who was the first Bishop of Périgueux. The sixth-century chapel was replaced by a larger church which was consecrated in 1047 but devastated by fire in 1120. This in turn was replaced by a third great basilica, completed in 1173, constructed in the form of a Greek cross. Byzantine in style, and with five cupolas – recalling the Church of the Holy Apostles in Constantinople and St Mark's in Venice – this pilgrimage church became an important stopover for those on their way to Santiago de Compostela. St Front's tomb was destroyed, however, and the church severely damaged during the Wars of Religion. Having fallen into disrepair it was radically restored in the nineteenth century – some say disastrously – by Abadie, the architect of the Sacré Coeur in Paris.

The historic Old Town of Périgueux is a conservation area. The narrow streets with their cobbled gullies and elaborate doorways are a constant reminder of the town's medieval and Renaissance past. The Rue du Calvaire (shown here), north of the Cathedral of St Front, is typical; it has been sensitively restored and is kept closed to traffic, and its elegant hôtels particuliers (private houses) are still inhabited, not the inanimate exhibits of an urban museum. These houses were built and decorated by wealthy burgesses in the fifteenth and sixteenth centuries, a time of prosperity for the town.

EXCIDEUIL

Excideuil in Périgord Vert on the River Loue is a small busy town with a lively market, where truffles are sold in the winter months. The town is dominated by its château, sitting on its stump of rock. The two stone keeps, one built in the eleventh century and the other in the twelfth, are linked by a curtain wall. Alongside the medieval fortress, built by the viscounts of Limoges, stands the Renaissance château, once owned by the Talleyrand family, with turrets and mullioned windows. The church, dedicated to St Thomas, was once a Benedictine priory, but it was much restored and altered in the fifteenth century when it acquired a flamboyant south doorway. During the iron industry's heyday in this region, iron ore was worked in open pits here, but today the town relies on its thriving trade in walnuts and fruit.

NEAR HAUTEFORT

It is time for the *vendange* at this small vineyard outside Hautefort. Where the number of vines does not really call for the use of expensive machinery, a farmer's neighbours will invariably offer to help with the grape-picking, expecting nothing in return except help with their own harvest and perhaps a good supper. This has been the pattern for centuries. As the grapes are picked they are brought to the *moulin* for pressing, their sugar content assessed by an experienced palate. Whether or not the vintage will be a good one is never predicted until the grapes are picked; the farmer's experience tells him that anything can happen until the moment of harvesting and indeed it is not unknown for a sudden summer hailstorm to ruin the crop. The wine produced from these rows of vines will be for domestic consumption, *vin ordinaire*, but good-quality *appellation contrôlée* wines are produced in the *département* for both the home market and for export.

CHÂTEAU DE JUMILHAC, JUMILHAC-LE-GRAND

The nineteenth-century illustrator Gustave Doré thought the roofscape of the Château de Jumilhac the most romantic in France. A fortress built by the Knights Templar once stood here; it was extensively altered, however, in the sixteenth century, when the wealthy ironmaster Antoine Chapelle acquired it and had the château constructed of the local schist, a hard stone, difficult to work – hence the rather grim, undecorated and prison-like aspect of the façades. The roof more than compensates for this restraint: pepperpot turrets, pinnacles, chimneys and towers are united in a sea of slate, surmounted by a selection of locally cast lead figurines depicting birds and angels, Cupid, cabbages and men. Inside the château is the room of 'La Fileuse', the spinner; this chamber was once occupied by the unhappy wife of Antoine II of Jumilhac who, suspected of infidelity, was confined to her room, where she passed her days in spinning and painting.

RIVER AUVÉZÈRE, NEAR LA FORGE-D'ANS

The river Auvézère provided ideal power sites for driving the furnace bellows and power hammers of the iron industry, that has a long history in the Dordogne. The smelting of iron reached its peak in the eighteenth century when French participation in the Seven Years' War increased the demand for armaments. Access to supplies of iron ore was easy and charcoal for firing the furnaces was abundant locally as the ironmasters owned large tracts of forest and employed their own charcoal-burners. At Château de la Forge-d'Ans are the remains of the house and forge built by the ironmaster Festugière, who came from Les Eyzies. Many villages in the area are suffixed by 'd'Ans', in honour of a Flemish nobleman from Ans to whom the medieval seigneur of nearby Hautefort gave his daughter in marriage.

THE DORDOGNE VALLEY
AND THE SOUTH

**THE DORDOGNE AT
CASTILLON-LA-BATAILLE**

In the fading light of a summer's evening, local fishermen discuss their catch and prepare to head for home. Fish abound in all the rivers of the Dordogne and fishing, although subject to strict controls, is a popular pursuit both for pleasure and for profit. Trout, in season from March to September, are a much prized catch while many other species are common in the Dordogne's clean waters, notably eels, carp and pike. All these contribute to the richly varied regional cuisine, so that even tiny fish such as gudgeon may end up on the dining table, crisply fried and eaten with the fingers.

On the western edge of the Dordogne, just inside the *département* of Gironde lies the town of Castillon-la-Bataille on the banks of the river. A battle was fought here in 1453 that effectively put an end to the Hundred Years War. The constant political instability provoked by this protracted period of warfare, during which much of Périgord was passed back and forth between the French and the English, arrested the artistic and cultural development of the whole of Aquitaine but the intermittent nature of the warfare allowed for much building and for the development of the *bastide* towns. Périgord, especially the southern part, possesses many well-preserved *bastides*, being in effect a frontier territory between the lands held by the French and the English kings.

The name *bastide* derives from the French *bâtir*, meaning to build. The construction of these revolutionary new towns – fortified, walled and inhabited by freemen – had begun in the thirteenth century, primarily for economic rather than military reasons. With the rapid expansion of the wine trade in the region the foundation of these new market towns was potentially an extremely profitable proposition for the medieval landowner. Peasants were encouraged to take up residence, as traders or artisans, by being granted enviable privileges, not least their freedom from onerous feudal duties. Several *bastides* were thus simply named Villefranche. In return for his freedom, a house and a plot of land, and the protection offered by the town's walls, the new resident would lend his artisanal skills and provide the landowner with revenue in the form of rent and market tolls. The towns were actually founded by the king or his agent in partnership with the landowner and, in time of war, the support of the townspeople could be relied upon. During the years leading up to the Hundred Years War – and throughout the hostilities – many new *bastides* were built and existing ones were fortified. The French and the English both built *bastides*, all according to a common plan. The large arcaded market square with its covered *halle* lay at the centre of a rectangular grid with the streets running at right angles. Each house with its plot of land was of roughly equal size and shape, and the houses were generally built of wood, and separated by narrow gaps called *andrones* which helped reduce the risk of the spread of fire. In the square near the market hall stood the church, very often heavily fortified; it would act as a keep and would be the last place of refuge for the town's inhabitants when under attack. The right to trade came under strict regulation and each town had its own weights and measures and currency. The old scales used for weighing walnuts and chestnuts and the measuring vessels for grain may still be seen at Villefranche-du-Périgord and at Monpazier, one of the best-preserved *bastides* in the Dordogne. The need for defence increased as the political situation in the thirteenth century deteriorated and ramparts with fortified gateways were erected around the towns. These are still in evidence today at Domme, the most beautiful of all the *bastides*, set high on a rock above the Dordogne river.

Here in the southwest of the *département* the Dordogne flows between two distinct regions, the Landais to the north of the river and the Bergeracois to the south. The Landais, between the Isle and the Dordogne, is, as its name may suggest, an extension of the great forests of the Landes south of Bordeaux, but it has more in common with its northern neighbour, the Double. Here in the Landais the landscape is less wild but still sparsely populated; there is almost as much woodland, the native chestnuts increasingly ousted by the maritime pine, and only occasionally giving way to clearings where tobacco and fruit trees are being encouraged to grow. At the western extremity of the Landais, as it drops into the fertile valley of the Dordogne, the density of the population increases, and crossing the river into the great plain of the Bergeracois, one enters a region where the landscape exhibits great diversity. It is land that has long been inhabited by man who has used it, with its variety of soils and climates, to his best advantage. Plums and peaches flourish here as do field crops like maize and tobacco, but this is primarily vineyard country like neighbouring Bordelais. It is the vineyards, like that at Monbazillac where sweet dessert wine is produced, that brought prosperity to Bergerac. Once an important port serving Bordeaux and a stronghold of the Protestant faith, today Bergerac is a busy agricultural market town, the centre of French tobacco production. The Bergeracois is a large plain but it is by no means featureless, being adequately furnished with hills; some of these, like Beaumont-du-Périgord, served as ideal defensive sites for *bastides* and indeed it is in this region that they proliferated.

Limeuil, upriver from Bergerac, is a delightful old walled village built on a steep hill overlooking the confluence of the Dordogne and the Vézère. Limeuil marks the point where three regions meet: Périgord Blanc, the Bergeracois and Périgord Noir. Périgord Noir is bordered to the north by the Vézère and to the south by the departmental boundary. The region is covered by dense forest, mainly oak but also chestnut and pine and juniper scrub, giving the landscape the appearance of darkness from which it derives its name. The region is also known as the Sarladais after its capital, Sarlat, a beautifully restored medieval and Renaissance town that has survived more or less intact from the seventeenth century. It is a centre for the marketing of walnuts and that speciality of the Dordogne, *foie gras*.

The rich alluvial soils of the river basins were as attractive to early man as they are to his modern counterpart. The lower Vézère valley provided prehistoric man with a plentiful supply of game and an abundance of naturally formed caves and rock shelters called *abris*. Evidence of continuous occupation since prehistoric times has indeed been found here. Les-Eyzies-de-Tayac on the Vézère has been dubbed 'the capital of prehistory' for it was here that the skeletons of Cro-Magnon man were found. Further up the Vézère at La Roque-Saint-Christophe is what is effectively a troglodyte village of caves in the sheer cliff face; the caves are linked by steps cut into the rock, high above the river. The most important site is upriver near Montignac at Lascaux, where some schoolboys, searching for their lost dog, discovered the now world-famous caves, decorated with paintings of bison, ibex, bulls, deer and horses.

Like so much of the *département* the rolling hills of the Sarladais were once clothed in vines but the vineyards were never replanted after the nineteenth-century phylloxera crisis. Sarlat was fortunate in having its trade in truffles, walnuts and *foie gras* upon which to fall back, and today it has a little light industry and tourism to bolster its economy. What perhaps is most noticeable in this region of the *département* is the effect of agriculture on the appearance of the land, the well-cultivated valley plains lying in marked contrast to the oak-clad hillsides. Poplars line the river banks and fields of maize and golden sunflowers are interspersed with strips of dark-green tobacco plants. Here the Dordogne makes its great arcing loops called *cingles* – like the one at Trémolat – and the bridges crossing the river gently reflect in the more peaceful waters.

As well as its *bastides* the Dordogne valley has an ample share of great châteaux like the vast medieval fortress overlooking the river at Beynac-et-Cazenac, which was once captured by Richard Coeur de Lion, and the twelfth-century Château de Castelnaud facing it from the opposite bank. Here, too, and along the valley of the Vézère, are to be found charming Romanesque churches like the near-perfect example at Saint-Léon-sur-Vézère.

The higher reaches of the Dordogne are across the border in the *départements* of Lot and Corrèze, no longer in Périgord but in the ancient province of Quercy. The landscape is noticeably different, for here one is entering the country of the *causses*, the high limestone plateaux, sparsely covered with poor pasture grazed by sheep. En route to the arid *causses* one passes through Souillac, with its splendid Romanesque abbey church, a town once made prosperous by its river trade with Libourne downstream: boats laden with timber for the wine trade would return to Souillac carrying salt. The beauty of the vernacular architecture at Autoire is a match for anything that Périgord can display, and the church of Beaulieu-sur-Dordogne with its masterpiece of Romanesque sculpture, the spectacular pilgrimage town of Rocamadour and the mighty château at Castelnau are equally hard to rival.

SAINT-MICHEL-DE-MONTAIGNE

East of Castillon and to the north of Montcaret is the château of Saint-Michel-de-Montaigne. The original château, birthplace of the essayist Michel Eyquem de Montaigne, was destroyed by fire in 1885. Little of that building remains, but the tower that housed Montaigne's private apartment was saved, and incorporated into the nineteenth-century Neo-Gothic château – the present building. On the ground floor is his chapel, on the second his bedroom and on the third his library, bereft of books but with rafters decorated with quotations from Plutarch and Seneca. Montaigne owned extensive property in Bordeaux but it was to the château and estates here that he was always drawn. He died here in 1592, famous as a man of letters and renowned for his judicious attempts at mediation during the Wars of Religion. Such was the esteem in which he was held that his heart was buried in the chancel of the twelfth-century church in Saint-Michel itself.

CHÂTEAU MONBAZILLAC

Château Monbazillac sits on a limestone plateau surrounded by vineyards, overlooking the valley of the Dordogne and the town of Bergerac to the north. Planted by monks in the eleventh century, the vineyards flourished, due to the demand for wine from Bergerac merchants and exiled Protestants. The château, a felicitous blend of medieval and Renaissance styles, was built by Charles d'Aydie from 1550 and, for all its martial appearance, was never a fortress, but more the home of a prosperous country squire. During the Wars of Religion Monbazillac, like Bergerac, was staunchly Huguenot, and the château now houses a Protestant museum. Since 1960 the château has been owned and restored by the Cave Coopérative de Monbazillac who continue to produce the fine dessert wine for which the region is justly famous.

ISSIGEAC

Issigeac lies in the Banège valley to the southeast of Monbazillac. Once completely walled, it is an attractive small medieval town, largely unspoilt, with winding streets of half-timbered houses interspersed with the occasional Gothic *hôtel*. As an ecclesiastical dependency of Sarlat, much of the building was commissioned by successive bishops who made the town their summer residence. The Gothic parish church, with an octagonal belfry supported by graduated angle buttresses, was built at the behest of Bishop Armand de Gontaut-Biron between 1498 and 1519. It was damaged both by the Huguenots and during the Revolution but it has now been restored. Facing the church is the Bishops' Palace, the vast Château des Évêques, which was built in 1699 by François de Salignac, uncle of Fénelon – the author of Télémaque. Flanked by brick-turreted square towers, it now houses the town hall.

BEAUMONT-DU-PÉRIGORD

Founded in 1272 for the English King Edward I by his seneschal of Guyenne, Luke de Thenney, Beaumont is one of the best-preserved *bastides*. In homage to Henry III, Edward's father, it was built in the shape of an H, and as its name suggests, occupies a hilltop site, ideal for defence. Some fifty years after its foundation, as the political situation deteriorated in the early fourteenth century, the town was encircled by a wall. The massive church, dedicated to St Front, would have served as the last defensive stronghold for the beleaguered townsfolk; during a siege, a well beneath the church would provide water for both the people and their animals. Extensive restoration in the nineteenth century removed some of its military features, but four fortified towers remain. The west façade has a more soothing effect: the porch, surmounted by an elaborate Gothic balcony, is decorated with ornate carving.

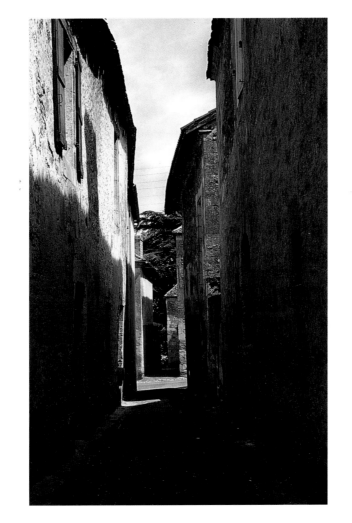

Edward I granted the town a market hall in 1289, and it stood in the square – on the south side – until 1864 when it was demolished. Shops with arcades known as *cornières* once lined this square on all sides and, indeed, some still exist, while only one of the town's sixteen original gateways remains more or less intact – the Porte de Luzier. Many of the houses lining the town's narrow streets, which cross each other at right angles, date – wholly or in part – from as early as the thirteenth century. Where rebuilding has taken place the original dimensions have been adhered to, giving the town a sense of continuity stretching back to the Middle Ages.

SAINT-AVIT-SÉNIEUR

In the sixth century St Avitus, former soldier turned hermit, founded a chapel here; dedicated to the Holy Virgin, it was later to be demolished by the Normans. The altar of the vast, austere and rather gloomy church that dominates an otherwise charming medieval village was consecrated in 1117 by Guillaume d'Auberoche, Bishop of Périgueux. The following year the mortal remains of St Avitus were disinterred and transferred to the church, now dedicated to his memory. The Augustinian abbey established south of the church was destroyed by the Protestants in 1576; all that remains to be seen is part of the chapterhouse and the ruins of a cloister. Excavation works have uncovered the foundations of the monastic buildings, however, and traces of a primitive Romanesque church, and many of their finds are displayed in the local museum.

MONTFERRAND-DU-PÉRIGORD

This pretty medieval village appears to tumble down the hill upon which it is built, rising above the valley of the Couze. During the Revolution Joseph Lakanal was sent to Bergerac as governor of the province and, upon his orders, the medieval château was largely destroyed. During the Wars of Religion it was the hiding place for the head shroud of Christ when Cadouin abbey – where the venerated relic was usually housed – came under threat of destruction by the Huguenots. There is great architectural diversity here for a village of this size. Dominating the square is a sixteenth-century covered market with fine limestone supporting pillars, and there are some fine Renaissance houses. The nineteenth-century church was built to replace the delightful Romanesque chapel which still stands in the cemetery surrounding it.

MONPAZIER

Of all the *bastides* of Périgord, Monpazier is perhaps the best known and it remains the most complete. It was founded in 1285 on behalf of Edward I by his seneschal, Jean de Grailly, in a partnership agreement with Pierre de Gontaut, Seigneur of Biron. The site upon which it is built was an empty hilltop above the river Dropt and from here road traffic from the south into Périgord could be controlled. The walls that once surrounded the town were pulled down and used to fill the moat, but the two entrances with their fortified gates remain. The church, dedicated to St Dominic, is fortified and retains much of its thirteenth-century character, although it was much restored and modified in the fifteenth and sixteenth centuries.

Monpazier's history is turbulent. During the Hundred Years War the town was pillaged alternately by the French and the English and, during the Wars of Religion, the town was captured by the Huguenots' leader, Geoffroi de Vivans. The deprivations that followed the Wars of Religion led to two brutally suppressed revolts by the peasants known as the *Croquants*. In the revolt of 1637 the *Croquant* leader Buffarot was captured and broken on the wheel in the market place. Built on a rectangular grid with streets at right angles, the town centred on the market square, where the restored sixteenth-century covered market hall – complete with its medieval measuring vessels – still stands. The square is surrounded by beautifully preserved, low, pointed-arch arcading, passing beneath the galleried houses.

CHÂTEAU BIRON

South of Monpazier, strategically sited on the borders or Périgord and Agenais, Château Biron sprawls imposingly atop its limestone outcrop. Biron was the hereditary seat of the Gontaut-Biron family, who were responsible for the harmonious assemblage of buildings created from the twelfth to the seventeenth centuries. The last Marquis of Biron was forced, through financial strictures, to sell the château and it is now under the control of the *département*, which is undertaking maintenance and restoration. The village, nestling within and below the confines of the fortress, owes its existence to the château. The beautiful sixteenth-century chapel is built on two storeys: the lower chapel serving as a parish church, while the upper tier, the seigneurial chapel, was used exclusively by the family.

VILLEFRANCHE-DU-PÉRIGORD

This medieval *bastide* town stands near the border of Périgord and Quercy. It was founded by Alphonse de Poitiers in 1261 and assigned to Edward I in 1287, but little of the original structure remains. The grid pattern of its streets is still evident, however, and its arcaded square and covered market, still exist. During the Wars of Religion Villefranche was Catholic while nearby Monpazier was Protestant. Unbeknown to each other, the inhabitants of both towns chose the same night to attack and loot their rival. Taking different routes both parties found the opposing town undefended, allowing them to loot to their hearts' content. The next day the truth of the situation revealed itself and, by mutual agreement, everyone returned to their homes and everything was restored to its rightful owner.

BELVÈS

The medieval fortified town of Belvès, its name a corruption of *belle vue*, is built on a promontory giving fine views over terraced gardens to the valley of the Nauze below. This is one of the principal walnut-producing areas of the country and Belvès is a centre for this flourishing trade. Walnuts are sold at the Saturday market held in the Place d'Armes, close to the fifteenth-century covered market hall, alongside the remnants of the medieval pillory. Fine Gothic and Renaissance houses are crammed within the town walls that also serve to protect the château, with its square twelfth-century keep. Today the château houses a museum devoted to the walnut.

CADOUIN

Robert d'Abrissel founded the magnificent Abbey of Cadouin for the Cistercian order in 1115, in a clearing in the Bessède Forest. Consecrated in 1154, the church is austere, a reflection of the Cistercian's dislike for ostentation. During the Middle Ages it became a place of pilgrimage, renowned for possessing the head shroud of Christ, brought from Antioch by a Périgordin priest returning from the first crusade. When its safety was threatened during the Hundred Years War it was moved to Toulouse, where it attracted thirty thousand pilgrims, when it was first displayed. Disputes over the shroud's ownership arose and only the combined intervention of the Pope and Louis XI effected its return to Cadouin. The economy of the town took a dramatic downturn when, in 1934, the shroud was revealed as a fake.

The prosperity brought by the pilgrims to Cadouin and the generosity of Louis XI and successive monarchs allowed for the rebuilding of the cloisters. Work was started in 1468 and continued until the middle of the sixteenth century; Flamboyant Gothic and Renaissance styles were combined, with much intricate carving and elaborate decoration, all in contrast to the sobriety of the church. These cloisters survived the Wars of Religion and the Revolution, coming under the wing of the State in 1839.

CINGLE DE TRÉMOLAT

The view from the road high above the north bank of the Dordogne at Trémolat encompasses the spectacular horseshoe bend or *cingle*. This broad meander was, to the French writer André Maurois, 'one of the wonders of the world'. The river makes its leisurely loop beneath steep white cliffs and is bordered to the south by a patchwork of fertile arable fields and meadow land. On the horizon rise the gentle hills of Bergerac and Monpazier. The village itself, with its twisting streets, sombre twelfth-century fortress church and delightful Romanesque chapel in the cemetery, is perhaps most memorable for being the setting of Claude Chabrol's gruesome film, *Le Boucher*.

LIMEUIL

The town of Limeuil, with its network of closely packed medieval streets, has long been inhabited. In 1909 remains of a Gaulish settlement were found here. It owes its name to the Romans to whom it was *lemoialum*, a place planted with elms. The town's natural defensive position – perched on a steep hill – and important strategic situation, overlooking the junction of two rivers, inevitably led to its extensive fortification in the Middle Ages; part of the rampart walls and three huge town gates may still be seen.

LIMEUIL

At the summit of the hill are
the ruins of the thirteenth-
century château where Henri
de la Tour, Vicomte de
Turenne, directed military
operations during the Wars of
Religion and where the Prince
de Condé's mistress, Isabeau
de Limeuil, also lived. Once
there was an arsenal here and,
until the nineteenth century,
the houses with their steeply-
pitched tiled roofs were
inhabited by boat-builders and
weavers. The domed church of
St Martin, consecrated in 1194,
lies in the valley below,
founded by Richard Coeur de
Lion and dedicated to the
martyr Thomas Becket. It has
been allowed to fall into
woeful disrepair, but is now
being restored by the Amis de
St Martin.

At its confluence with the
River Vézère at Limeuil the
Dordogne is relatively shallow,
flowing quickly over gravel
banks – an enticing spot for
fishermen, swimmers and
canoeists. The well-cultivated
valley plains, planted with a
variety of crops and recently
established fruit trees, contrast
with the distant wooded hills
of Périgord Noir. Where the
two rivers meet the *pont coude*
('elbow bridge') stands, in
effect a pair of round-arched
stone bridges joined almost at
right angles, one crossing each
river.

**GISEMENT DE LA
MADELEINE,
NEAR TURSAC**

Near this small town on the
Vézère, with its fortified
Romanesque church, there is
evidence of much earlier
habitation. During the final
period of the Upper
Palaeolithic Age, the *abri*
(shelter) at La Madeleine was
inhabited by cave-dwellers. In
this, the age of cave painting,
so-called Magdalenian man
had become proficient in the
manufacture of sophisticated
tools and weapons. Such
materials as were available –
bone, ivory and horn – were
skilfully made into needles,
blades and scrapers, while
finely worked flint was used
for arrow- and spear-heads.
Many of these finds, excavated
from the *gisement*, the
accumulated debris of the *abri*,
are exhibited in the museum of
prehistory at Les Eyzies.

NEAR SIREUIL

Sireuil, a few kilometres from
Les Eyzies, is a small town
with a domed Romanesque
church and a seventeenth-
century iron foundry. Nearby
is this Gaulish village, a group
of vaulted dry-stone huts
known as *bories, garriottes* or
cabanes, which date back to
the time of the Roman
occupation of Gaul. Built for
shepherds to use, they are
roofed with *lauzes*, split slabs
of limestone.

NEAR SIREUIL

Madame Segondat's house, La Bosse, where she lives with her son Paul, has altered remarkably little since it was built – around the time of the construction of the Château de Commarque. Neither have the pace and pattern of the Segondats' lives changed very much over the years. To many they would appear to possess few creature comforts, their splendid longcase clock the only display of wealth; yet they want for nothing. Their small farm produces *un peu de tout* all year round, geese and chickens patrol the farmyard and home-baked bread and wine pressed from home-grown grapes are never in short supply.

CHÂTEAU DE COMMARQUE, NEAR MARQUAY

The gaunt ruins of the Château de Commarque stand, barely accessible, on the south bank of the River Beune. Early in the twelfth century the château was given by its owner, Gérard de Commarque, to the Templars, in order to raise money for a crusade. It passed from them to the Hospitallers and was later bought by the Baron of Beynac, who gave it to one of his sons. But by the beginning of the fifteenth century it was under English occupation. How it came to be largely destroyed is disputed. In the sixteenth century the King ordered its demolition but according to local tradition it was destroyed by fire. Some of the vast complex does still stand, notably the heavily fortified keep, the chapel and part of the living quarters.

CHÂTEAU DE LAUSSEL, NEAR MARQUAY

From the shutterless windows of the ruined Château de Commarque one can look across the valley of the Beune to the altogether more domestic Château de Laussel. Built during the fifteenth and sixteenth centuries in the Renaissance style, this elegant building has been restored and is now inhabited. An important prehistoric deposit was found a little way along the valley, including the famous 'Venus of Laussel', a low-relief carving from the Aurignacian period, which is now to be seen in Bordeaux Museum. On the walls of the prehistoric shelter at nearby Abri du Cap Blanc there are also large-scale bas-relief carvings of bison, deer and horses, dating from the Magdalenian period.

LA ROQUE-SAINT-CHRISTOPHE, NEAR TURSAC

North of Les Eyzies in the lower valley of the Vézère, beside a tranquil stretch of the river, is a settlement that saw continuous habitation from prehistoric times until the eighteenth century. The galleries of caves, on five interconnecting levels, with staircases cut from the rock, reach to a height of over 250 feet. The terraces were fortified in the tenth century against the Normans and used during the Hundred Years War, but the fortress was destroyed during the Wars of Religion. Nearby is the Pas du Miroir, a pathway hewn from the rock face, so called because of the reflection gained from the river that once flowed at the foot of the cliff.

SAINT-LÉON-SUR-VÉZÈRE

Lying within a loop of the river, the beautiful village of Saint-Léon-sur-Vézère possesses this exquisite Romanesque church, built of honey-coloured stone and roofed with darker *lauzes*. Formerly a Benedictine priory church attached to the abbey in Sarlat, it stands on the site of a Gallo-Roman villa, its two-storey belfry reflected in the river. The church exterior is unornamented, its interior simple and austere, with traces of frescoes on the chancel and some stone sculpture around the walls. Its beauty lies in the perfect balance of its curves and verticals, in the harmony of the rounded apse and chapels with their pointed stone caps beneath the square belfry with its *lauze*-covered spire. In the cemetery on the outskirts of the village is a fourteenth-century *lauze*-roofed chapel that once served as a *Lanterne des Morts*, a temporary resting place for the dead.

Buildings are not the only relics of the past to be found in the villages of the Dordogne. This Citroen *traction avant* (on the left) in Saint-Léon-sur-Vézère, revolutionary in its time and still retaining its stylish appearance, passes its last years in the company of other redundant vehicles, including a horse-drawn trap, in the shade of a spreading walnut tree.

CHÂTEAU DE BELCAYRE, NEAR SAINT-LÉON-SUR-VÉZÈRE

Despite its warlike aspect, the extensively restored Château de Belcayre was never seriously intended to have a defensive role. Turrets, arrow-slits and machicolations are more decorative than functional. Built in the fifteenth century on a site once occupied by a fortress, the château stands on a limestone outcrop directly above the Vézère. Freda White in her *Three Rivers of France* relates the tale of financial caution exercised by the owner of the nearby Château de Losse, famous for its remarkable echo: '...the seigneur of Belcayre, finding himself in a tight place, went to his neighbour to borrow money. Losse, a canny man, cried to the echo: *"Moussur de Belcayre ei teu buon pagaire?" "Gaire! Gaire!"* ("Is Monsieur de Belcayre a good payer?" "Watch out!") answered his echo, and poor Belcayre did not get his loan.'

MONTIGNAC

The town of Montignac, built astride the Vézère, was once an inland port, reliant upon the river trade, and galleried medieval buildings line its quays. When the painted caves at nearby Lascaux were discovered quite by chance in 1940 the town turned to tourism for its livelihood and the annual 100,000 visitors brought prosperity with them. The closure of the caves because of the deterioration of the paintings heralded a commercial downturn for the town but it still appears to thrive. The ruined château dates from the twelfth century; once a seat of the counts of Périgord, it was partly destroyed in 1398 by Maréchal Boucicaut the French commander defeated at Agincourt. On the terrace behind stands the splendid Hôtel de Bouilhac, bristling with domes, balconies, chimneys and pointed slate roofs. Eugène Le Roy, author of *Jacquou le Croquant*, lived here, and the local museum bears his name.

CHÂTEAU DE LA GRANDE FILOLIE, NEAR SAINT-AMAND-DE-COLY

Between Montignac and Saint-Amand-de-Coly lies the Château de la Grande Filolie, sheltering in a small wooded valley. The château is a picturesque amalgam of seventeenth-century Renaissance manor and fortified fifteenth-century house, linked by a polygonal tower. The mullioned windows, discreet chimneys, turrets and roofs of *lauzes* combine harmoniously to achieve a unity, despite the differences in style and proportion of the various buildings. The château forms a complex with a chapel and a group of farm buildings that once comprised a virtual village community in itself, secure and self-contained.

SAINT-AMAND-DE-COLY

In the small village of Saint-Amand-de-Coly, in a little valley off the main valley of the Vézère, stands the most impressive fortified church in the Dordogne. Part of an Augustinian abbatial complex, it dates from the first half of the twelfth century and was erected on the site of an earlier building thought to have been founded by St Amand in the seventh century. Surrounding the church are high defensive walls, dwarfed in turn by the sheer scale of the huge fortified west front. The massive fourteenth-century bell tower has walls four metres thick and contains a defensive chamber into which the villagers could retreat from their homes – huddling around the church – for safety. Under the eaves around the roof ran a pathway; fire could be directed from here onto the enemy below. Despite these defences the abbey and its church did not remain invulnerable. Driven out by the Huguenots in 1575, the monks were eventually banished forever during the Revolution.

SAINT-CYPRIEN

The village of Saint-Cyprien spreads over its hillside site on the right bank of the Dordogne, northwest of Beynac-et-Cazenac. The massive church, which dominates the village, is dedicated to St Cyprien, who reputedly founded the village in the sixth century; it formed part of the abbey established here for Augustinian canons. The sturdy Romanesque belfry-keep dates from the twelfth century, but the heavily restored main body of the church, which houses the heart of Christophe de Beaumont, Archbishop of Paris, is fourteenth-century Gothic.

Attractive stone houses with steeply pitched roofs of slate, tile or chestnut shingle jostle for space in the steep streets around the church. Close to the village are two châteaux worthy of note: the moated, sixteenth-century Château de Fages to the north, which stands in ruins having been burnt by German soldiers hunting for the Resistance; and the Château des Milandes, on the other side of the river. The rich alluvial soils of the Dordogne valley are ideal for growing tobacco and the Régie Nationale des Tabacs, the State Tobacco Board, has taken over the former abbatial buildings in the town to use them as a depot and warehouse. On their arrival in January or February, bales of dried tobacco are stored and processed here before despatch.

SAINT-VINCENT-DE-COSSE

This delightful medieval village lies between Saint-Cyprien and Beynac-et-Cazenac on a beautiful stretch of the Dordogne its name taken from the early Christian martyr, Vincent of Agen. Legend has it that in an attempt to bring Christianity to the area Vincent incurred the displeasure of the local druids who had him spreadeagled, staked to the ground, flogged and finally beheaded. Buildings are of the mellow local stone with mullioned windows; some are roofed with *lauzes* and have *outeaux*, small triangular openings which are characteristic of the region. These not only give ventilation to the loft space but also offer access to the owls which prey upon small rodent pests living inside.

THE DORDOGNE, FROM CHÂTEAU DES MILANDES

None of the soil of the fertile valley plains escapes cultivation. The soil and climate allow the mixed arable farms to grow a rich diversity of crops. Cereals and fodder crops are planted in strips alongside fruit trees, and the Dordogne has also become the foremost producer of strawberries in the country. Tobacco is an important cash crop for the Dordogne farmer too, despite the labour-intensive nature of its cultivation. The Château des Milandes, built in 1489 by François de Caumont for his bride, stands on the east side of the river. It has been much restored. This work has in part been undertaken by the château's most famous chatelaine, the cabaret performer Josephine Baker, who made it her retirement home – together with her multi-racial family of adopted children. Despite having been the highest-paid entertainer in Europe, however, she was eventually forced by the prohibitive cost of restoration to sell the château.

BEYNAC

The forbidding *château-fort* of Beynac stands spectacularly atop the cliff, overlooking a beautiful twist of the Dordogne as it passes serenely through meadowland below. Perched 450 feet above the picturesque medieval village, the château was built in the twelfth century; it belonged to the Beynac family until 1195 when it was taken forcibly by Richard Coeur de Lion. Richard allowed it to be used by the brutal courtier–soldier Mercadier, who wreaked havoc in the locality. The château was dismantled in 1214 by Simon de Montfort during his crusade against the Cathar heretics, only to be rebuilt by the lords of Beynac. It became the seat of one of the four great baronies of Périgord where the *parlement* met during the Middle Ages, and remained a French stronghold during the Hundred Years War.

The village of Beynac cannot escape the domination of the château, a splendid example of military architecture, which has been well restored by the Beaux Arts. Where not protected by a sheer drop there is a double perimeter wall, a double moat and a barbican. The Beynac-Beaumont family, who still own the château, have improved and added to the structure over the centuries. The Salle des États, where the Périgordin Estates sat, is a most impressive feature, with its fine barrel vaulting; the adjacent chapel has fifteenth-century frescoes depicting members of the Beynac family and the Last Supper.

CAZENAC

The other village in the
Beynac-et-Cazenac commune,
Cazenac – less than a
kilometre away – is free from
any sense of oppression,
occupying as it does a hilltop
site with fine views of the
surrounding wooded
countryside. Its simple little
fifteenth-century church with
a roof of *lauzes* is furnished
largely with clear glass, its
spacious vaulted interior being
thus filled with light.

THE DORDOGNE FROM
CHÂTEAU BEYNAC

From the ramparts of Château
Beynac, high above the
Dordogne, this splendid
panorama unfolds – the river
valley and the wooded hills
beyond. Upstream lies
Beynac's great rival, the
formidable Château de
Castelnaud. The Château de
Fayrac in the foreground, lying
low on the hillside, is
altogether more pacific. Built
of yellow limestone, the
remains of its fourteenth-
century buildings are within
the inner courtyard, reached by
crossing a drawbridge. Much of
the château dates from the
fifteenth and sixteenth
centuries having once been the
home of the Protestant Vivans
family, but it underwent
restoration in the nineteenth.
Pepperpot towers, gables and
crenellations give it a romantic
air, in marked contrast to the
austerity of Beynac which
stands opposite.

LA ROQUE-GAGEAC

Pressed into the cliff towering vertically above it, La Roque-Gageac was once an inland port; boats used regularly to ply the river, heading west to Libourne and the Atlantic coast laden with locally produced wine and timber for barrel-making, and returning – carrying provisions – to Souillac and beyond. One of the most beautiful villages in the Dordogne, its houses of mellow stone reflect in the tranquil river. A cliff fall in 1956 demolished many of the houses sheltering below, killing some of the occupants, but careful rebuilding has left the new houses indistinguishable from their older neighbours. At the western end of the village the nineteenth-century Château de la Malartrie appears fifteenth-century in style. To the east is the Manoir de Tarde, once the family home of the noted nineteenth-century sociologist, Gabriel de la Tarde, a descendant of the astronomer, mathematician and local chronicler Jean Tarde, who was born at La Roque-Gageac in 1561.

CÉNAC

Cénac faces La Roque-Gageac from across the Dordogne and here, too, the villagers derived their livelihoods from the river. Slightly west of the village is a small Romanesque church, all that remains of the Priory of Saint-Julien, which was founded by Aquilanus, Abbot of Moissac, in 1090, and completed in the first part of the twelfth century. The priory was largely destroyed by the Protestants during the Wars of Religion, only the chevet – the semi-circular eastern end – surviving unharmed. The nave and transepts were rebuilt in the nineteenth century. But the church's interest lies in the wealth of naturalistic Romanesque carving which still survives. Inside, the capitals bear carvings of plants and animals, and graphic representations of biblical stories; outside, the carvings on the cornice around the roof of each apsidal chapel are more grotesque: a lion devours its prey and a pig consumes two human heads, while a contortionist – to ward off evil – turns his backside to the viewer.

DOMME

Domme was founded in 1281 for the King of France, Philippe le Hardi. The most beautiful of the *bastide* towns of Périgord, it occupies a hilltop site hundreds of feet above the Dordogne. Domme's history is one of violence and occupation: it changed hands repeatedly during the Hundred Years War, and then, a Catholic stronghold during the Wars of Religion, it was captured by the famous Protestant captain, Geoffroi de Vivans, in 1588, in an act that combined great courage with military trickery. The precipitous cliff face above the river, known as the *barre*, was believed to be impossible to climb and was therefore left undefended. A party of thirty men scaled the *barre*, and created a disturbance in the marketplace, so that Vivans and his troops positioned on the other side could burst in and take the town.

Domme is built on an irregular plan to allow for the uneven terrain but the streets are classically arranged on a grid. Today two winding roads lead into the town: one through the Porte des Tours, where the Knights Templar were held prisoner in the fourteenth century; the other through the Porte del Bos. The charming, well-restored houses are constructed of sandstone of a perfect ochre hue. The numerous external staircases or balconies, festooned with vines and decorated with potted geraniums and begonias, make the town a delight for the summer visitor.

CHAPELLE DE CAUDON, NEAR DOMME

Geoffroi de Vivans, having stormed and captured Domme for the Protestant cause, burnt down the church and descended to Cénac below, where he devastated the priory. Vivans held Domme for four years until 1592 and during this period of Protestant occupation the Catholic community were prevented from celebrating Mass. Cut into the cliff on the river road just to the west of Domme, the Chapelle de Caudon was built by the hounded Catholics in order that they might worship there until Domme was retrieved from the Protestants. Now disused, the little church nevertheless remains a poignant reminder of the years of intense religious strife in the region.

CHÂTEAU MONTFORT

Château Montfort stands on a rocky promontory above its own *cingle*, where the River Dordogne makes a massive loop around the little village of Turnac. Built in a strategically important position, it has a history of sieges and violent conflict. It acquired its name from the legendary Simon de Montfort, leader of the crusade against the Cathar heretics; he seized it from Bernard de Casnac and promptly burnt it to the ground. The château was subsequently rebuilt but partially destroyed three more times. The château consequently comprises a mixture of styles. The main tower dates from the fifteenth century, the wings from the sixteenth, but the majority of the romantic elements – the turrets, machicolations and dormer windows – are part of the nineteenth-century restoration. Today the château and its grounds are private.

SARLAT

Sarlat, once the capital of Périgord Noir, lies in an unremarkable valley nine kilometres from the Dordogne. Its unadvantageous position allowed it to escape the depredations of the Normans and, being near neither roads nor railways, it was also spared the typical excesses of nineteenth-century restoration. The greatest indignity suffered by the town came with the building of the Rue de la République in 1837; known locally as La Traverse, it cruelly slices through the heart of the medieval town, giving little impression of the charm and beauty that lie beyond its shopfronts. Sarlat's most renowned citizen, Étienne de la Boétie, was born here in 1530 in a house that may still be seen. His fame emanates from both his relationship with Montaigne and his own writing. His impassioned plea for liberty, *Contr'un ou Discours de la servitude volontaire*, became the inspiration for Rousseau's *Du Contrat Social*. La Boétie died in 1563.

The Hôtel de Grézel, its elegant staircase tower furnished with a fine ogee-arched doorway, dates from the fifteenth century and survived the Wars of Religion, during which Sarlat – by then a wealthy mercantile town – remained steadfastly Catholic. Geoffroi de Vivans captured and held it for three months, during which time priests were murdered and holy relics destroyed. And some years later the Huguenot commander, the Vicomte de Turenne, laid siege to the town but he was repulsed and Sarlat was left largely undamaged. While the Revolution left the buildings of Sarlat more or less untouched, Napoleon's centralization of government curtailed further expansion of the town.

SARLAT

By the nineteenth century the
economic prosperity enjoyed
by the town in medieval and
Renaissance times had gone,
its economy now depending on
the trade in walnut oil and
truffles. Slowly the town slid
into a decline until, in 1964,
rehabilitation began in earnest.
Many of the houses, built of
ochre stone, turreted and
gabled, often with roofs of
lauzes, have been impeccably
refurbished, and there is a
wealth of fine architectural
detail to be seen.
Distinguished Renaissance
hôtels jostle with earlier half-
timbered houses in the narrow
twisting streets. The walnut
trade still thrives; geese are
still sold at the Saturday
market in the Place des Oies;
and the town has deservedly
become one of the great tourist
attractions of the Dordogne.

SARLAT

Standing in the former
cemetery of the Cathedral of St
Sacerdos, the enigmatic
building known as the
Lanterne des Morts is the
strangest to be found in Sarlat.
It was built in 1180, reputedly
to commemorate the
miraculous curing of the sick
by St Bernard when he visited
Sarlat to preach against the
Albigensians in 1147.
Resembling a large, blackened
sugar loaf, its function is
unclear. There was an ossuary
beneath the tower and it seems
probable that the chapel above
was used as a sepulchral
chamber. Possibly it was used
for the many victims of the
plagues that devastated
Sarlat's population in the
fourteenth and fifteenth
centuries; a light in the lantern
would have warned the
unsuspecting of the presence
of infection. In the
seventeenth century the
bourgeoisie of Sarlat used the
tower as a meeting house,
where they would elect their
consuls.

CHÂTEAU DE PUYMARTIN

The Château de Puymartin, a few kilometres northwest of Sarlat, was built in the fifteenth and sixteenth centuries on fourteenth-century foundations. What one sees today is the romantic nineteenth-century idea of how a medieval château should look. Much restoration and rebuilding of the Renaissance structure was undertaken by Léon Prouin, a Bordelais pupil of the great Viollet Leduc, but it remains both interesting and picturesque. Built of golden stone and roofed with *lauzes*, its twin turrets, huge machicolated keep and curtain walls contrast with its tranquil setting. During the Wars of Religion it was a Catholic stronghold, serving as a headquarters for the general who was commissioned to retrieve Sarlat from the Huguenots.

In the summer visitors may take a guided tour of the splendid interior of the Château de Puymartin. The hexagonal chapel – with its star vaulting – is the oldest part of the château. The furnishings and decoration are particularly fine: eighteenth-century Aubusson tapestries hang in the state room, which has a beautiful parquet floor, and in the main hall the Renaissance chimneypiece is painted with *trompe l'oeil* effects. Much of the furniture has always been in the house, dating from the Louis XIII and Louis XV periods. The faint-hearted should take note that the house is said to be haunted by a mysterious 'white lady'.

NEAR GROLÉJAC

The rearing of geese fits in well with the system of polyculture practised on many small farms in the Dordogne and most farmers will keep at least a small flock. The goose is not usually roasted and eaten whole, as it is too fatty, but almost every part has a use, culinary or otherwise. The neck is served stuffed with the chopped gizzard, and the coagulated blood is made into pancakes known as *sanguettes*. Even the beak and the feet are eaten and the copious fat is an essential ingredient in much of the regional cuisine. In November the geese are taken indoors for the *gavage*. They are force-fed three times a day for three to four weeks with a mixture of warm boiled maize and fat. As a result the goose's liver becomes unnaturally large, up to six times its normal size, producing the *foie gras* much prized by gourmets. The geese are killed and the livers, weighing around a kilo each, are sold at market in time for Christmas.

The highly prized truffle is a variety of fungus, *Tuber Melanosporum*; it grows symbiotically on the roots of oaks, just below the soil surface. It was the *haute cuisine* of the royal houses of eighteenth- and nineteenth-century Europe that led to the widespread popularity of this 'black pearl of Périgord', renowned for its delicate yet pronounced flavour. Truffle production reached its peak in Périgord in the latter part of the nineteenth century: the country's vines were almost totally devastated by phylloxera and many of the region's *vignerons* replanted with 'truffle' oaks. Production rose to between 100 and 150 tons a year. The First World War saw the collapse of truffle-culture; by the 1960s, annual production had fallen to three tons; today the cultivation of truffles is again on the increase. Those fortunate enough to have truffles on their land search for them in winter, often aided by a keen-scented dog or sow, and sell them at market, where they command a high price.

CARSAC-AILLAC

Just southeast of Sarlat the delightful church of Carsac, built of golden stone, its nave and pointed belltower roofed with *lauzes*, shelters in a little wooded grove. Built in the twelfth century, the church suffered at the hands of the English during the Hundred Years War, but it was restored in the late fifteenth and sixteenth centuries. More recently, in the 1940s, some particularly sensitive restoration work was undertaken, which contrived to blend the modern with the Romanesque in an entirely successful way.

One enters the porch with its five lines of coving, passing into the broad-aisled nave which was restored after the Hundred Years War and given its fine ogive-vaulting to the nave and chapels. Further restoration in the Renaissance added some fine bas-relief carved bosses, corbels and capitals. One central boss is carved with the head of the architect, Antoine de Valette, while another shows the infant Hercules grappling with a snake, and the capitals are carved with a variety of stylized flora and fauna. The twentieth century gave the church its stained-glass windows and the modernistic Stations of the Cross, carved by Leon Zack to the text by the poet and dramatist, Paul Claudel. Zack also gave the church an engraving on stone of St Teresa, and one of his windows depicts St Caprais, the patron saint of Carsac.

SOUILLAC

The town of Souillac does not lie in the Dordogne, but just over the border in the *département* of the Lot, and here one is no longer in Périgord but in the ancient province of Quercy. The town, situated at the confluence of the Borrèze and the Dordogne, grew up around the Benedictine abbey. Having suffered during the Hundred Years War, this abbey was destroyed during the Wars of Religion, but fortunately the domed Romanesque church survived, its Byzantine air reminiscent of the Cathedral of St Front in Périgueux. The great dome is roofed with *lauzes* and is surmounted by a lantern turret, while the smaller dome and the rounded bays beneath, with their arches and blind arcading, have warm tiled roofs.

The interior of the church is spacious, elegant and simply decorated, apart from the magnificent carving of the west doorway, brought inside the church for protection from the Huguenots and reinstated there. The splendid Romanesque carvings not only illustrate scenes from the life of the monk Theophilus who, according to legend, made a pact with the devil, but depict fantastic beasts and the prophets Isaiah and Joseph as well.

SOUILLAC

Tobacco grows well in the rich alluvial soil of river valleys and the *départements* of Lot et Garonne and Dordogne are the two major producers in France. The cultivation of tobacco calls for labour-intensive methods with the plants requiring much attention in the summer months – regular weeding, disbudding and the application of fertiliser. Harvesting too is a time-consuming operation often lasting from mid-August until early September. Individual plants are cut in the early morning and allowed to wilt before being carried to the *séchoir*, a purpose-built, ventilated drying house, or are simply hung upside down to dry under the eaves of the farmer's barn. Having been left to dry for up to sixty days, the leaves are then bundled up and sent to one of the government depots for processing. The restored former abbey at Souillac now serves as a tobacco warehouse for the area.

NEAR SALIGNAC-EYVIGNES

Despite the trend towards mechanization and specialization in agricultural production, many Dordogne farmers still choose to maintain more traditional methods of farming. On this mixed arable farm potatoes grow in serried ranks alongside the farmer's vines in their full flush of early summer growth. What better method of earthing up your potatoes in the confines of these narrow rows than by using a horse-drawn plough, precise and leisurely, the farmer and his wife in total harmony with the environment, and keeping alive a centuries-old tradition of agricultural practice. This is not to say that the Dordogne farmer is not progressive. When the time comes to harvest his grapes, he may well employ one of the futuristic *vendange* machines, that strip the vines in a fraction of the time it would take to harvest the crop by hand.

SALIGNAC-EYVIGNES

The imposing Château de Salignac was built – and is still owned – by the Salignac family, who count among their number the writer and Archbishop of Cambrai, François de Salignac de la Mothe-Fénelon, of whom some relics are on show inside. The terraces and ramparts that encircle the château date from the twelfth century and are still largely intact. The château itself was built over a period stretching from the twelfth to the seventeenth centuries. The severity of the façades, emphasized by the flanking round and square towers, with their pointed caps, is relieved by the mullioned windows and warm hues of both the stone and the *lauzes* used to roof the whole of the château complex. In the town, which hosts a busy market, there are the remains of two thirteenth-century buildings, a convent and the Abbey Sainte-Croix.

CHÂTEAU DE LA TREYNE, NEAR BELCASTEL

The Château de La Treyne is built on a cliff that rises perpendicularly above the Dordogne, ten kilometres upstream from Souillac. The enormous central keep is all that remains of the original structure, which was built by the Rouffilac family in the fourteenth century, for the château was burnt down by the Catholics during the Wars of Religion. Most of the present building dates from the seventeenth century, when it was rebuilt and restored by the de la Ramière family. It once housed a fine collection of Italian and Spanish furniture which, when left to the *département*, was transferred to the château at Bourdeilles. Today La Treyne serves as a luxury hotel.

BELCASTEL

Three kilometres to the west
of La Treyne the remarkable
jumble of buildings that
comprise Belcastel look down
from a dramatic cliff-top site,
three hundred metres high.
Below the Dordogne and the
Ouysse converge to run as one
stream. Only the chapel and
the eastern part of the main
wing date from medieval
times, the castle being
substantially the result of
nineteenth-century
restoration. The chapel and the
terraces are open to the public
and the view obtained from
above the ancient ramparts
makes the climb well
worthwhile.

ROCAMADOUR

The spectacular village of
Rocamadour clings to the
precipitous rock face above the
gorge of the tiny river Alzou.
The village takes its name
from St Amadour, whose
identity remains a mystery.
After the discovery of an
uncorrupted corpse there in
1166, miracles began to occur.
Up until the Reformation
Rocamadour was one of the
most important pilgrimage
centres in Europe: Henry II
came twice and received a
miraculous cure; and penitents
would make their painful way
to the shrine of the Black
Virgin, climbing the 216 stone
steps on their hands and knees,
bound in chains, to receive
absolution. The village and the
shrine were sacked repeatedly
during the Hundred Years War
and the Wars of Religion but,
after a long decline,
Rocamadour was revived as a
place of pilgrimage in the
nineteenth century.

CIRQUE DE MONTVALENT

Below Carennac the Dordogne cuts through between the Causse de Martel in the north and the Causse de Gramat in the south. *Causses* are high limestone plateaux, thinly covered with stunted oaks and grass, grazed by sheep and sparsely populated. From the Belvédère de Copeyre, with its iron Calvary, a splendid panoramic view of the Cirque de Montvalent may be gained. Here the rich pasture and arable farmland, broken up by small groves of poplars and walnut trees, is cut by the sweeping arc of the river. All around the circular plain wooded cliffs rise to the *causse* above, creating this spectacular natural amphitheatre.

The favourable soils of the flat basins and great plains between the *causses* of Gramat and Martel, in the region known as Haut Quercy, mean that a wide variety of crops are grown there. Strawberries and *reines claudes* (greengages) are cultivated near Carennac and, alongside the great meadows, vines and fields of tobacco thrive. Walnuts make a large contribution to the region's economy and here, beneath the magnificent trees in late September, the back-breaking task of collecting the walnuts, is already under way. Women and children seem to be given the job of gathering the nuts which have been allowed to fall, a job best done early in the morning, before the farm animals have had a chance to glean. Some of the walnuts will go to the mill where they will be pressed for their oil, but mostly they are sold at market near Christmas time.

MARTEL

In the *département* of Lot, built upon the limestone *causse* to which it gives its name, the medieval town of Martel is known as the 'town of seven towers'. Charles Martel, grandfather of Charlemagne, founded the town. Having checked the Muslim invasion of Europe by defeating the Saracens at Poitiers in 732, he pursued them into Aquitaine, and it was at this place that, some years later, he finally overwhelmed them. He built a church in commemoration of his victory, and around it the town grew up. During the twelfth century Henri Court Mantel was in dispute with his father, King Henry II of England; his allowance was cut off and his lands given to Henri's brother Richard Coeur de Lion. Henri, short of funds, plundered and desecrated the surrounding abbeys and the shrine at Rocamadour. But he was then racked with guilt and remorse and fled to Martel. Here he received, by messenger, timely forgiveness from his father, before he died of fever.

The Hôtel de la Raymondie, once the law courts and now the town hall, is a fine mansion built by the Viscount of Turenne between 1280 and 1330. A tower stands at each corner of the building, an architectural feature much in favour in Martel. This fine medieval *hôtel*, flanked by a round tower, has been further embellished with a splendid Renaissance doorway of carved stone which surrounds the heavy oak door studded with iron, adding a touch of elegance and grandeur to a rather forbidding exterior.

MARTEL

Martel is an architectural gem of a town. Everywhere you turn there are fine fourteenth- to sixteenth-century houses, and the whole town centre is 'listed'. Once fortified, the remains of its protective double perimeter walls can still be seen. The fourteenth-century church of St Maur was fortified too, its two watchtowers and massive belfry being flanked by buttresses and provided with loopholes. In the porch, meanwhile, is a fine Romanesque tympanum carved with the Last Judgement. Narrow streets lined with medieval houses radiate from the Place des Consuls, in the centre of which stands the eighteenth-century covered market, its wooden superstructure supported by stout stone pillars.

CARENNAC

The village of Carennac on the Dordogne developed around the prior-deanery, founded in the tenth century and attached to the abbey at Cluny in the eleventh. Medieval and Renaissance houses, built of golden stone and with roofs of mellow brown tiles, congregate around the much-restored deanery and, through a fortified archway, one catches sight of the splendid twelfth-century carved portal of the Romanesque church of St Pierre. The tympanum above the doorway has at its centre a serene Christ in Majesty in a mandorla, an almond-shaped aura; His right hand is raised in blessing, while He holds the Book of Judgement in His left. He is encircled by the symbols of the four Evangelists and flanked by representations of the Apostles. These delightful carvings are attributed to artists of the Toulouse School who, in the twelfth century, produced some of the most beautiful carved doorways in France.

CARENNAC

When the senior prior of Carennac died in 1681, he was succeeded by his nephew, François de Salignac de la Mothe-Fénelon. Known simply as Fénelon, the theologian and writer was appointed as tutor in 1689 to the young Duc de Bourgogne – Louis XIV's grandson. It is commonly held that it was here that Fénelon wrote his great masterpiece about Ulysses's son, *Les Aventures de Télémaque*, and thus tradition has dubbed this peculiar elongated building Télémaque's Tower. The novel was written for the edification of the young duke and was never intended for publication, but it was published clandestinely by one of Fénelon's enemies. Construed as a direct criticism of the monarchical government of Louis XIV, the book led Fénelon – already out of favour with the court – to be banished to spend the remainder of his life in disgrace at Cambrai.

LOUBRESSAC

From its hilltop eyrie, the fortified village of Loubressac commands a splendid view: the valley of the Dordogne and the little River Bave stretch away, punctuated by the town of Saint-Céré and the towers of Saint-Laurent-les-Tours. At the end of the spur on which the village was built stands a fifteenth-century manor house, rebuilt and given its pepperpot roofs in the seventeenth century. The village has many fine old houses like these; built of irregular, hand-cut stones and with pointed roofs of baked brown tiles, they are basking here in the afternoon sun of a late summer's day. One has the outside staircase typical of the houses of Quercy. Shutters of chestnut or oak help to keep the houses cool in summer and warm in winter, which can sometimes be harsh.

AUTOIRE

On the edge of the Causse de Gramat the little village of Autoire nestles at the bottom of a valley. Above the village a series of waterfalls cascade down beneath the Cirque d'Autoire, a splendid rocky amphitheatre clad in stunted oaks. Périgord and Quercy have some of the most beautiful rural architecture in France and nowhere is this more apparent than in Autoire. The houses here were built for once prosperous *vignerons* and the substantial *manoirs*, built to stand the test of time, have far outlived the vineyards, which suffered badly in the phylloxera epidemic of the nineteenth century. The Romanesque church stands in the centre of the village and all around on rising ground cluster the elegant turreted houses, timber-framed or built of pale limestone from the Segonzac quarries, their dormer windows jutting out from steeply-pitched roofs.

Solid and substantial, roofed in a mixture of flat and round tiles, this elegant *Quercynoise* house in Autoire sits encircled by the rugged amphitheatre above. At the corner of the building is the *pigeonnier* (dovecote) with its pyramidal roof of *lauzes*. In Périgord dovecotes are comparatively rare, being the privilege of the nobility, but in Quercy, a region of small landowners, few houses are without one. In the past little livestock was raised here and pigeons provided not only a valuable supplement to the winter diet but a source of precious fertilizer for the farmer's fields as well.

CHÂTEAU DE MONTAL

The beauty of the perfect Renaissance Château de Montal belies its tragic past. Jeanne de Balsac d'Entraygues commissioned the finest craftsmen and artists to build and decorate this delightful country house for her son, Robert de Montal, who was in Italy fighting for François I. When Robert was killed in battle, his mother issued instructions that the window from which she vainly looked for his return be blocked up, and that around it should be inscribed the plaintive message, *'Plus d'espoir'* – 'No more hope'. At the end of the nineteenth century the château was stripped of its furnishings and decorative fixtures, which were sold off by the unscrupulous owner. The château passed into the hands of a M. Fenaille who, in an act of supreme philanthropy, tracked down and purchased the missing treasures, restored the house and gave it to the nation. In the background can be seen the ruins of Saint Laurent-les-Tours.

SAINT-CÉRÉ

Saint-Céré lies in the Bave valley beneath the watchful gaze of the ruined towers of the fourteenth-century fortified château of Saint-Laurent-les-Tours. The number of fine houses dating from between 1400 and 1600 is a reflection of the prosperity enjoyed by the town after the Viscounts of Turenne granted it rights of trade and commerce. The town came under the protection of the château of Saint-Laurent and was left largely untouched by the Hundred Years War. In the oldest part of the town, around the Rue du Mazel, solid Renaissance *manoirs* – turreted and with fine doorways – compete for space with older, more modest buildings. This attractive house, painstakingly restored in every detail, is a fine example, with its exposed timber framework in-filled with patterned bricks.

CHÂTEAU DE CASTELNAU

The great Château de Castelnau gazes out majestically over the oak-clad landscape of the ancient province of Quercy. The château's mighty red ironstone ramparts and towers survey the confluence of the Dordogne and the Cère from a rocky promontory between the river valleys. The barons of Castelnau were the most powerful in Quercy and in about 1080 Hugues de Castelnau built the round keep. The fortress complex, with its fortified perimeter wall, was developed during the Hundred Years War, at one time housing a garrison of 1,500 men and 100 horses, but the château was abandoned and neglected in the eighteenth century and badly damaged by fire in 1851. It was restored between 1896 and 1932 by the tenor Jean Mouliérat, who left it and his collection of fine furniture and tapestries to the nation at his death.

BEAULIEU-SUR-DORDOGNE

Beaulieu-sur-Dordogne lies in the *département* of Corrèze on the right bank of the Dordogne. A religious community was founded here as early as 855 when the Archbishop of Bourges, Rudolph of Turenne, changed its name from Vellinus to Bellus Locus – Beau Lieu – literally, beautiful place, so impressed was he by the town's location. The abbey church and the chapter house are all that remain of the Cluniac abbatial buildings of the twelfth century. The Wars of Religion caused the monks, who had strayed some way from the path of righteousness, to desert the abbey, and they were succeeded in 1633 by the strict Benedictine Congregation of Maurists. The monastery buildings were repaired and order restored to the religious community, which thrived until the monks were driven out by the Revolution.

BEAULIEU-SUR-DORDOGNE

The former abbey church of St Peter was built by masons from Toulouse, whose work may be seen in the great Romanesque churches of Carennac, Souillac and Moissac. The church is large and well proportioned but its true treasure is the carved south portal, completed in 1125. On either side of the porch are mutilated carvings depicting Daniel in the lions' den and the Temptation of Christ. Above the door is an elaborate tympanum with a vigorous carved representation of the Last Judgement. A beneficent Christ in Majesty holds out His arms in welcome above two angels, who herald the Day of Judgement with trumpets. Christ is flanked by the Apostles and below them the dead are seen rising from their graves. On the lintel the fallen sinners are harried and devoured by many-headed monsters and chimeras.

In addition to its splendid abbey church Beaulieu possesses some fine buildings, some dating back to medieval times. Particularly beautiful is the twelfth-century Chapel of the Penitents with its unusual wall-belfry, which stands on the bank of the river, mirrored in the water. Charming old houses cluster around the church and opposite the west face is this remarkable Renaissance building, shuttered against the afternoon sun. On its exterior a veritable gallery of carved medallions and figurines in niches is cut into the stone. The purpose behind this embellishment is unknown, but it certainly enlivens an otherwise plain façade.

PHOTOGRAPHER'S NOTES

The first thing that strikes you on entering the region of the Périgord in the south-west of France, is how 'tree'd' the landscape becomes; not evergreens, but deciduous varieties of every shape and size. The second thing that strikes you is how warm, friendly and hospitable the inhabitants of Périgord are.

No other experience I had while making this book exemplifies the latter better than the morning on which I met Paul Segondat and his mother. For days I had been talking to the local people, and asking them if they knew of somebody still living according to the old traditions of the region. I repeatedly heard of a mother and her son living in the old *'fermette'* built into the side of a valley not far from the Château de Commarque, and dating, so it was said, from the same period. I had been given directions, and early one morning I found myself, against my better judgement, nervously traversing an oversized path – the kind the French candidly refer to as a *'chemin'*.

Finally the car arrived at a small courtyard, where geese and chickens held sway. Madame Segondat was sitting on an old piece of timber in the barn, busy with her needlepoint. I cautiously went over and enquired as to whether it would be possible to meet her son, and indeed whether I might take their photograph. She seemed some-what perplexed but, after a few moments' thought, raised her middle and forefingers to her mouth and let out one of the shrillest high-pitched whistles I had ever heard. I fully expected to see a pack of hounds appear to dismiss this unwanted observer. Moments later, however, that aggravating early morning sound the French have all but mono-polized was to be heard whining in the distance. Within seconds a pint-sized figure on an evidently cannibalized machine appeared over the bluff. With his shotgun riding pillion, and a rather tired-looking beagle in hot pursuit, Paul Segondat arrived with a squeak and a bump. To my relief, as I explained the purpose of my visit, his face beamed, showing a selection of teeth that would make the most unobservant of den-tists see red. He ushered me inside, but stopped short of the threshold to comment with some pride on the thickness of the walls. They were certainly impressive, leaving a good yardstick only a few inches to spare. We sat astride a rustic bench beside the breakfast table to discuss the true age of the house and the family tree; on the table lay wine, cheese and yesterday's bread. Within seconds the loaf was removed, and replaced with a steaming wholemeal straight from the oven. This was truly the Périgord.

For this photograph, and for many of the others in this book, I have used Leica cameras, because I find their image quality unsurpassed. I would like to thank both Graham Wainwright of Leeds Film and Hire, London, and Graham Rutherford of Fuji Film for their help and generosity. I would also like to thank Michael Dover of Weidenfeld & Nicolson for 'believing' in me, Colin Grant, the editor of this volume, for his perseverance and support – a good helmsman is hard to find – and last, but not least, my wife Isabelle and daughter Zoë who waited so patiently.

BIBLIOGRAPHY

Bentley, James, *A Guide to the Dordogne* (Viking 1985)

Bentley, James, *Life and Food in the Dordogne* (Weidenfeld and Nicolson 1986)

Beresford, Maurice, *New Towns of the Middle Ages* (Lutterworth Press 1967)

Brook, Stephen, *The Dordogne* (George Philip 1986)

Duby, Georges and Mandrou, Robert, *A History of French Civilization* (Weidenfeld and Nicolson 1965)

Escande, J.-J., *Histoire du Périgord* (Laffitte Reprints 1980)

Escande, J.-J., *Histoire de Sarlat* (Laffitte Reprints 1976)

Fayolle, Gérard, *La Vie Quotidienne en Périgord aux temps de Jacquou le Croquant* (Hachette 1977)

Lands, Neil, *A Visitor's Guide to the Dordogne* (Moorland Publishing 1983)

Law, Joy, *Dordogne* (Macdonald 1981)

Michelin, *Dordogne: Périgord-Limousin*, Green Guide (4th edition, 1984)

Nebolsine, George, *Journey into Romanesque* (Weidenfeld and Nicolson 1969)

Oyler, Philip, *The Generous Earth* (Hodder and Stoughton 1950)

Oyler, Philip, *Sons of the Generous Earth* (Hodder and Stoughton 1963)

Penton, Anne, *Customs and Cookery in Périgord and Quercy* (David and Charles 1973)

Scargill, Ian, *The Dordogne Region of France* (David and Charles 1974)

Secret, Jean, *Le Périgord: Châteaux, manoirs et gentilshommières* (Editions Tallendier 1966)

Sullam, Joanna and Waite, Charlie, *Villages of France* (Weidenfeld and Nicolson 1988)

White, Freda, *Three Rivers of France* (Faber and Faber 1952)

INDEX

Page numbers in *italics* refer to illustrations. Places mentioned in the captions are not indexed, apart from those shown in the pictures.